GOD AND THE REFEREE
UNFORGETTABLE GAA QUOTATIONS

Eoghan Corry is a writer and columnist. Three of his previous books on sports history – *Viva*, *Catch and Kick* and *Kingdom Come* – went to number one in the Irish bestsellers. He has storylined the sports museum in Croke Park and is the former sports, business and features editor of three national newspapers.

GOD AND THE REFEREE

Unforgettable GAA Quotations

Eoghan Corry

Hodder Headline Ireland

First published in 2005 by Hodder Headline Ireland

A CIP catalogue record for this title is available from
the British Library.

ISBN 0340 839767

Typeset in Berling Antiqua and Schindler by Hodder Headline Ireland
Printed and bound in Great Britain by Clays Ltd, St Ives plc.

Hodder Headline Ireland
8 Castlecourt Centre
Castleknock
Dublin 15
Ireland

A division of Hodder Headline
338 Euston Road
London NW1 3BH

Contents

For my daughter Síofra
and in memory of Peggy MacMahon (1922–1996)
of Clahanmore and Larkfield Grove.

Neither of whom were ever stuck for a pithy phrase,
witticism or piece of poetry to suit every occasion.

'As Saint Paul said—'

As *God and the Referee* went to print, the GAA's 118th All-Ireland Championships were in full swing. Debates, disputes and discussions were taking place about forthcoming matches, though the past was not forgotten either, with time and space given as required for inquests and comment on the braves that were history.

Yes, we are a race of compulsive talkers and I cannot remember a time when it was difficult to find people willing and able to express opinions on any one of a myriad of topics.

But I do not think that Ireland was always like this. We have all heard of the Golden Age when the country was known as the Island of Saints and Scholars. I cannot imagine the Irish of that era talking animatedly about sport – and hurling was in vogue at the time – they would have been too reserved from the constant pursuit of scholarship and prayer.

Didn't Saint Patrick spend forty days in silence at the top of a mountain in Mayo! Would he have held out if Mayo had been billed to play in a Connacht final during his retreat?

I have a theory that the staging of All-Ireland championships for the first time in 1887 transformed the people of Ireland into loquacious beings with an instant expertise in judging sport.

People were beginning to travel to more distant places because that century provided a new mode of transport, the railway, and its existence had a lot to do with the gradual development of sport.

It is said that travel broadens the mind and generates opinionating, and those packed trains that served the GAA so well for so long heard many a quotable phrase that would have felt at home beside their kith and kin in Eoghan Corry's wonderful compilation, taken from many sources that make this book such a wonderful bridge between the distant past and the living present.

To the legions of GAA followers, there is always a certain mystique about the players who go out in search of All-Irelands and other honours. In this, his latest book, Eoghan succeeds in getting us enveloped in the same mystique by introducing us to the sport of hurling and the heroes who played it in an age 2,500 years before Christ. He imprisons us with a quote about those times written by P.J. Devlin some four score years ago: 'The men of Ireland were hurling when the gods of Greece were young.'

From then on, through the book's 300-plus pages, the reader is treated to a menu of quotes that offers the greatest level of variety on this side of heaven. In turn they can be seen as challenging, balanced, partial, memorable, ridiculous, humorous, political, racist, descriptive, educational and even offensive.

But then somebody penned them in the first place or delivered the words in reality or imagination and accordingly were there for Eoghan to weave into his wonderful cocktail. Naturally newspapers, memoirs and observations detailed in letters form the base for a good deal of information about the early days of the GAA and the centuries that preceded it.

And let us not belittle the part played by the many ballads that first saw the light of day as humble green sheets bearing welcome words peddled by nomadic entrepreneurs in the fairs and happy gatherings in the Ireland of old.

But as the twentieth century wore on, those sources increased in volume and generosity, and both Eoghan and the GAA were fortunate that media such as radio and television appeared on the scene to supplement the wonders of the written word. The author draws on them, and of course I am flattered to read a few of my own words included alongside others.

For me the most pleasant aspect of reading through this book was the frequency with which I 'met' again the characters and personalities of the GAA that I was honoured to know through the passing decades. But it provided plenty of enlightenment also on other matters and people.

Never again fear the question, 'Who said that?' – *God and the Referee* surely has the answer.

And by the way, my favourite quote from the entire luminous litany is that of a Cork woman at the funeral of Christy Ring – 'It's a mortal sin to be burying a man like him.'

Comhgháirdeachas leis an bhfoireann a chuir an ráiteas-fhéasta seo ar pháirc na súl agus na gcluas. Fearfar fáilte roimhe.

MICHEÁL Ó MUIRCHEARTAIGH

Ancient Games

When writing came to Ireland in the fifth century, a game called iomáin popped up in the earliest manuscripts and later, when the authors of the sagas wished to endow their heroes with great strength, dexterity and athletic expertise, they used mastery of the skills of iomáin as a metaphor. The poets also recorded great games and feats of valour on the playing field. The Tailteann Games, an athletics festival sponsored by the symbolic High King of Tara in Meath, and two other festivals in Kildare and Wexford are also mentioned – all of which forms an impressive body of literature. The Battle of Moytura might not be dated accurately by people writing 4,500 years after the event, but that scarcely matters. All of these sources assumed that readers were familiar with the game, assumed to be hurling or a close relative.

'The men of Ireland were hurling when the gods of Greece were young.'
P.J. Devlin. (c.1924).

'Ruad, with 27 sons of the courageous Mil, sped westwards to the end of Magh Nuad to challenge an equal number of the Tuatha de in a hurling match. They dealt many a blow on legs and arms, till their bones were broken and bruised, and fell stretched on the turf and the match ended.'

From the 15th-century manuscript 'Cath Mhaigh Tuireadh Chung', an account of the Battle of Moytura, 4004 BC, translated by J. Fraser.

'He took his hurling stick of bronze and his silver ball, and he would shorten his journey with them. He would strike the ball with the camán and drive it away from him. Then he would catch his hurling stick and his ball. He went to the place of assembly of Emainn Mhacha where the youths were. There were thrice fifty youths led by Follomain mac Conchubuir at their games on the green of Emain. The little boy went onto the playing field in their midst and caught the ball between the legs when they cast it. Nor did he let it go higher than the top of his knee nor lower than his ankle. And he pressed the ball between his two legs. And he carried the ball away over the goal.'

'Táin Bó Cúlaigne' from *The Book of Leinster*, translated by O'Rahilly (1970). *The Book of Leinster* was probably written around 1180 by Aed mac Criomtháinn at an Nuachabáil, near the townland of Stradbally in County Laois.

'It is ordered, enacted and statuted that what so ever man is at no time to… occupy the hurling of the little ball with hockey sticks or staves, nor use no handball to play without the walls, but only the great football.'

The Statue of Galway (1527).

'The Commons of the said land of Ireland, who are in divers marches of war, use not henceforth the games which men call hurlings, with great clubs at ball along the ground (*horlinges oue grounds bastons a pilot sur la terre*), from which great evils and maims have arisen, to the weakening of the defence of the said land.'

The Statues of Kilkenny (1366).

'The new settlers are speaking Irish, playing hurling and copying the customs of the natives.'

A letter of William Gerrarde (1578).

'Tully Fair next St Swithin's Day, the 15th of July, and always after, will be kept on that part of the lands of Tully next the Curragh. About three in the afternoon there will be a hurling match on the Curragh, between 40 men from each side of the Liffey for 30 shillings. A barrel of ale, tobacco and pipes will be given to the hurlers.'

The Flying Post (or *The Post Master*) (28-29 June 1709). This is the first newspaper reference to hurling.

When the cows are casting their hairs, they pull it off their backs and with their hands work it into large balls which will grow very hard. The ball they use at hurlings which they strike with a stick called commaan, about three foot and a half long at the handle. At this sport one parish sometimes or barony challenges another; they pick out 10 or 20 players from each side, and the prize is generally a barrel or two of ale. This commonly is upon some very large plain, the barer of grass the better, and the goals are 200 or 300 yards one from the other. Whichever party drives the ball beyond the other's goal wins the day. Two or three bagpipes attend the conquerors at the head and then play them off the field. At some of these gatherings two thousand have been present... They do not play often at football, only in a small territory called Fingal near Dublin the people use it very much, and trip and shoulder very handsomely.'

John Dunton, *Observations in Ireland* (1691).

'I divided my troops into small parties, placing at the strongest bodied men to resist the first shock, the nimble near at hand, and the corps de resistance to attend to myself. The enemy seeing the day lost at football attempted to retrieve their honour by strokes, which were altogether as fruitless for our discipline availed us as much at them as it had done at the ball.'

Dudley Bradstreet, describing a football match in Aughamore between Longford and Westmeath (1737).

'It is in the month of August that the playing of hurling commences. Each team is divided into three groups, the back (*arriere ou back*) guard the goal (*fourche*) and strive to prevent the ball (*balle*) from passing there. Another group is in front to prevent the enemy's ball repassing from their side, that is the middle, the third or the whip is on the field between their middle and their back to force the ball to pass under the goal. The game is played only in Munster and Connacht. In Leinster football is played. In Ulster Presbyterians are scandalised by Sunday play.'

Coquebert de Montbret, *Travels in Ireland* (1789–1791).

'The great game in Kerry and indeed throughout the south is the game of hurley, a game rather rare although not unknown in England. It is a fine manly exercise, with sufficient of danger to produce excitement, and is indeed, par excellence, the game of the peasantry in Ireland. To be an expert hurler a man must possess athletic powers of no ordinary character. He must have a quick eye, a ready hand, and a strong arm. He must be a good runner, a skilful wrestler, and withal patient as well as resolute.'

S.C. Hall, *Ireland Its Scenery, Character, etc.* (1843).

'The hurling matches in the province were the Olympic games of old Ireland: the athletes of Connacht would challenge the rival hurlers of Munster. County against county, but more frequently Bally against Bally came forth in mutual and picturesque defiance.'

Lady Morgan, *Memoirs* (1862), published 3 years after her death.

'And they have been killing each other ever since.'

England's King George V after being told that hurling dates to the Battle of Moytura in 4004 BC, while attending a hockey match in 1921. Quoted in T.S.C. Dagg, *History of Hockey* (1934).

Back Doors and Backchat

'The back door.' Coined by Micheál Ó Muircheartaigh in 1997.

Marty Morrissey: 'Why did they lose to Monaghan, then?'

Pupil: 'They were trying to lose, so they'd get through the back door easier.'

Conversation between Marty Morrissey and Conor Williamson, a primary school pupil from Ballyhegan.

'The qualifier system has made the All-Ireland harder to win but expectations in Kerry haven't reduced.'

John O'Keeffe (27 September 2003).

'If Offaly were so opposed to the back door as they like to assert, they could have stated, the moment they were beaten in the last three Leinster finals, "We are now out of the championship of this year, and will not be appearing in any championship fixtures until next year."'

Kevin Cashman, *Sunday Independent* (1993).

'There is a huge appetite out there among GAA followers for more inter-county games. The sad thing is that it took the GAA 117 years to even commence to cater for that demand.'

Eugene McGee, *Irish Independent.*

'No rest for the weakened.'

Irish Independent headline, on the new GAA back-door format, which still requires beaten teams to play the following week.

Ballads

Street ballads were the first newspapers of Ireland, and the feats of hurlers and footballers continue to be recorded in song and verse to modern times. It would be normal for two pages of *come-all-ye*s to appear in a provincial newspaper a week after a famous victory and some of the most catching are still sung today. The most famous GAA ballad of all was about someone who never played the game, except in his imagination.

'Sport with a dash in it/Clatter and clash in it/Something with ash in it/Surely a game.'

Phil O'Neill, 'The Game of the Gaels', first published in the *Cork Free Press* (1916).

'Oh my feet shall be swift as the white skin-drift/On the bay in the wintry weather,/As we run in line through the glad sunshine/On the trail of the whirling leather... So fashion a hurl from the fine young tree,/And give it the race of your blessing/'Twill fare right glad in the whirl of play/When the Southern lads are pressing:/And honour bestow on the dead below/The meadow our heels are spurning/Who fought for the fame of the Gaelic games/When the fire of their youth was burning.'

Neil Crawford, 'The Song of a Hurl' (1916).

'Without exaggeration, our goalers take their station/For the highest approbation they have won their victory/'Twas in no combination, or field association/But in rural relaxation on the plains of Ownabwee.'

Thomas Crofton Croker, 'The Carrigaline Hurlers' (1798–1854).

'The ash is king of the song I sing,/A song of sinew and brawn /A song for men – while men are men/The song of the brave Camán…The hopes and fears of a thousand years /Once more are pulsing there,/There's a rhythmic clash as ash meets ash,/ Men fleeter than flying fawn/'Tis the symphony of the old ash tree/The song of the brave Camán.

Peadar Kearney, 'Song of the Camán'.

'When from her sleep of ages renowned Tipperary woke/ Her sister, fair Kilkenny, right courteously she spoke/The Gaelic sun has risen, your champions call in fine/For Erin's olden glory, to clash camáns with mine/Moondharrig, Moondharrig, ye leaped into the fray/Moondharrig, Moondharrig, how gloriously that day/Moycarkey and Moondharrig, a stubborn fight ye fought/Moondharrig, Moondharrig, what wonder works ye wrought.'

J.B. Dollard, 'Moondharrig' (c.1915).

'At the great hurling match between Cork and Tipperary/ 'Twas played in the park by the banks of the Lee/Our own darling boys were afraid of being beaten/So they sent for bould Thady to Ballinagree/He hurled the ball left and right in their face/And showed those Tipperary boys learning and skill/If they came in his way sure he surely would brain them /And the papers were full of the praise of Thade Quill.'

Johnny Tom Gleeson of Ballinagree, north of Macroom, in a mock-heroic tribute to the Bould Thady Quill, allegedly a day-dreaming employee of the author, published in the *Duhallow Sportsman*. The ballad became popular when included in a Walton's *Instrumental Galleries*.

'Thus for an hour the battle raged/Hotter and fiercer they each engaged/Those stalwarts bold unknowing fear/Their county's honour alone held dear.'

Phil O'Neill, 'Cork vs Tipperary' (1913).

'What is your fear boys when Semple is with you/The gallant old captain who leads in the fray/Why should you doubt when you think of the past boys/That one word Dungourney should all trouble allay.'

'Ballad of 1909 Munster final'.

'Three nonpareils Kildare can claim/Honourable clean and manly/Their names can grace the hall of fame/Dempsey, Conneff and Stanley.'

Anonymous Kildare ballad (1919).

'Have you marvelled at the daring/The feats of skill you see/Have you wondered as they crash and sway and fall/Yet, they're up again and going/Hear the thousands shout in glee/ It takes a man to play it after all.'

Frank Doran (1929).

Ballads

'Many a fierce and well-fought field/Proved well their skill and brawn/For the hands behind the battle spears/Were trained at the camán.'

J.B. Dollard, 'Clash of the Camán'.

'Though Erin's old ranks have been broken/That once were the proud of the past/And bitter the words that were spoken/We know they no longer can last/For the spirit of old cannot perish/So in unity now let us join/To honour the hurlers of Ireland/And amongst them the men of Mooncoin.'

Phil O'Neill, 'The Men of Mooncoin', published in the programme for the Jim Droog Walsh benefit (5 September 1926).

'I sing you a song as we stream steam along/The well-filled special train/We're merry and bright and glad tonight,/Our colours on top again/The day is done, and Cork has won/And now we hold the sway/So join the cry and raise on high /For gallant old Cork Hurrah!'

Phil O'Neill.

'You have the Irish dances yet/Where is the Irish hurling gone/Of two such lessons why forget/The nobler and the manlier one.'

Anonymous ballad, inspired by Thomas Francis Meagher's plea to a Repeal meeting in Waterford, 'Hold on to your hurling' (c.1848).

'It brings us back the high renown/Of Gall and Finn the Fair,/To see them battle for the crown/Brave Kerry and Kildare.'

Liam O'Sheridan, 'The Gaels of Erin'.

"Tis a Kerryman's clear understanding/That, when to those colours he's true/He's wearing a mantle demanding/The best that a mortal can do/Their passing beyond has bereft him/But no Kerryman needs to be told/That a legacy grand they have left him/That's fashioned of green and of gold.'

Joseph Smyth.

'Love and praise we e'er accord/The men of might and brawn/Who foot the leather o'er the sward,/And held the stout camán.'

Phil O'Neill, 'The Gaels Beyond the Wave'.

'Every foreign game we now disdain/Golf, cricket and ping pong/Rugby and soccer in our midst/have flourished far too long/so true to name each Irish game/We'll pride in and we'll play/in bold young Ireland, Irish Ireland/Ireland boys hurrah.'

Gaelic Athlete (3 February 1912).

'A grand strike by Locky/Hurtles towards the square/Martin White flicks it out/to catch it will he dare/Yes, he turns around and strikes/A hard one for the poles/And even the great Conlon/Could not save that goal of goals.'

'Ballad of 1935 All-Ireland'.

'No more shall lime white goalposts soar tapering and tall/ Above the greatest goalman that ever clutched a ball/Nor yet he'll rouse the echoes of ash in native air/Nor heed the throbbing thousands tense with the pride of Clare.

'On the windswept hills of Tulla/Where Claremen place their dead/Four solemn yews stand sentinel/Above a hurler's head/And from the broken northlands/From Burren bleak and bare the dirge of Tommy Daly/Goes surging on through Clare.

'To think he'll never once again/Don with lithesome air/ The claret gold of Tulla/Nor the blue and gold of Clare/ Perhaps he'll play when feats are high/And heal the wounds of fight/God rest you Tommy Daly/On your windswept hill tonight.'

Bryan MacMahon, 'Lament for Tommy Daly', *An Ráitheacháin* (December 1936).

''Twas Beckett's grand goal that finished the fray/And Tubridy's pace was the talk of the day/But our backs were like granite where Weeshy held sway/Agus fágfaimid siúd mar atá sé.'

P.D. Mehigan, 'Ballad of the 1945 final'.

'And they'll oft retell the story/of the glory that was Lory's/ When Meagher graced the black and amber/Of Kilkenny by the Nore.'

Quoted in Pádraig Purseil, *The GAA in Its Time* (1982).

'The flags of Heffo's Army now/How limp they hang and lean/Their bearers stunned by dire defeat/By Kerry's young machine/The Dubs' young blood to silence hushed/By our gallant gold and green.'

'Ballad of 1975'.

'In the month of November/'twas a wild stormy day/I shut the front door and to town made my way/I met with a young man on the road I did go/And he told me the news of the gallant John Joe/He led Cavan to victory on a glorious day in the Polo Grounds final when Kerry gave way/In Croke Park the next year when our boys bet Mayo/Once again they were led by the Gallant John Joe.'

'The Gallant John Joe', tribute to John Joe Brady of Cavan, composed after his death on 21 November 1952.

'The men who founded the GAA/Would scorn the modern parasitic way.'

Anonymous ballad, collected by Jimmy Smyth.

'It's not a crown of diamonds/That speaks of fame untold/ But a treble crown of laurels/That speaks of fame untold.'

Ballad about Tipperary's victory in senior, junior and minor All-Irelands of 1930.

'He wears 16 stone and never forget/he has the heart of a tiger and the speed of a jet/Better keep your distance if want to grow/When you're playing on a man called Paddy Kehoe.'

'Ballad of Wexford' (1956).

'Now certain folk down South don't like us/They say our game is dour/"Well boys," I say, "don't ate the grapes/If you find they are sour."'

Patsy O'Hagan, the bard of Tyrone (2003).

'Give them a chance, if you stint them now, tomorrow you'll have to pay/A larger bill for a darker ill, so give them a place to play.'

Denis A. McCarthy, 'Give Them a Place to Play' (1921).

Bans and the Ban-Wagon

People who know nothing else about the GAA know that they banned foreign games and the British, including Northern Irish policemen and soldiers, from membership until long after the bans made much sense. Peculiarly, these issues were rarely debated within the GAA itself while the bans were in place. When they were, it led to some extraordinary high rhetoric and sharp exchanges.

'Any member who plays, attends or helps to promote rugby, soccer, hockey or cricket thereby incurs automatic suspension from membership of the Association.'
Rule 27 (as it then was).

'British soldiers, navy men and police shall not be eligible for membership of the GAA.'
Rule 26 (as it then was), later Rule 21.

'Members of the British armed forces and police shall not be eligible for membership of the Association. A member of the

Association participating in dances or similar entertainment promoted by or under the patronage of such bodies shall incur suspension of at least three months.'

Rule 21.

'Our rules prohibit the use of our grounds for any other games.'

Joe McDonagh, president of the GAA, *The Irish Times* (8 September 2001).

'Here is a nice kettle of fish. Policemen are members of the Metropolitan Hurling Club. Is it fair to shunt them without notice? The executive has brought itself into such a condition that contempt would be wasted on it. A body of men who are never done saying that they are non-political, introduce the boycotting system without notice, and in such a manner as to leave themselves open to the charge of being actuated by political animosities.'

Michael Cusack, *The Celtic Times* (5 March 1887).

'I call on the young men of Ireland not to identify themselves with rugby or Association football or any other form of imported sport which the GAA provides for self-respecting Irishmen who have no desire to ape foreign manners and customs.'

T.F. O'Sullivan of Kerry (1901).

'We should not even entertain a motion relating to foreign games until the National Flag flies over the 32 counties of a free and undivided Ireland.'

Motion from Tyrone before the 1947 Congress.

'A motion was carried unanimously, that the ban on RUC men and British soldiers should remain. The next item on the agenda was an application to the British government for increased grants for the GAA, and that too was carried unanimously'

Kevin Myers, *The Irish Times* (4 June 1998).

'The ones with their heads down at the rugby matches when the photographs were being taken were the GAA players.'

Eamonn Cregan, quoted in Brendan Fullam, *Hurling Giants* (1994).

'I would like every Irishman to play the game that most appeals to him and I have no sympathy with the policy of exclusion pursued by the Gaelic Athletic Association.'

Seán MacEntee, Fianna Fáil politician (1931).

'Traditional values provide ballast in an era of aimlessness and disillusionment.'

Seamus Ó Riain, GAA president (1965).

'It is that sense of allegiance to something permanent and enduring that has always been our strength. Our rules derive not only from a desire to organise health-giving exercise but from a determination to defend national values, traditions and aims. That is what has given an enduring vitality to the work of the Gaelic Athletic Association. This is the force which has forged the links that bind our members. At all times we shall continue to guard our pastimes that have enriched the national life.'

Dan O'Rourke of Roscommon, GAA president (1962).

'The GAA intends to delete Rule 21 from its official guide when the effective steps are taken to implement the amended structures and policing arrangements envisaged in the British–Irish peace agreement.'
Danny Lynch, GAA PRO (1998).

'If anyone thinks the games of the empire have a greater call on them than the games of his country, he is welcome to go to them.'
Tom Walsh, Kilkenny GAA chairman (1928).

'The motion [to remove the Ban] is not a proposal to rescind a rule but rather a proposition to alter the fundamental structure of the Association and to open the ranks to those who never accepted us for what we are.'
Pat Fanning, GAA president (1970).

'Let there be no sounding of trumpets as the rule disappears. Nor should there be talk of defeat. If victory there be, let it be victory for the Association.'
Pat Fanning, when the rule was removed by unanimous agreement (1971).

'The GAA inhibits Catholics from joining the Unacceptable RUC – Rule 21 is Catch 22.'
Con Houlihan, in a letter to *The Irish Times* (June 1998).

'People subject to an oath of allegiance to the Crown gaining admission to the GAA if the ban on the RUC and British Army were lifted. For generations national teachers and other public officials in Northern Ireland have given outstanding service to the GAA. Four GAA presidents came from that constituency – a constituency whose numbers were subject to an oath of allegiance to the Crown as a condition of their employment.'

Letter to *The Irish Times* (17 November 1997).

'It is essentially the GAA's problem that its good name continues to be held to ransom by a conservative rump.'

Irish Times editorial (9 April 2001).

'There are good historic reasons why Rule 21 was introduced and those reasons still exist. The British army and the RUC continue to intimidate and harass nationalists in general and members of the GAA in particular.'

Letter to *The Irish Times* (1 July 1998).

'Narrow Win for Fearful Bigotry.'

Sunday Independent headline (8 April 2001).

'Croker an Icon to Sporting Bigotry.'

Irish Independent headline (9 April 2001).

'The rule is this: if the ball is oval and you throw it backwards, it is a foreign game which may not sully the Gaelic acres of Croke Park. But if it is oval and you throw it forwards, it is perfectly acceptable and may grace the hallowed turf at any time. Is there any sense in this?'

Kevin Myers, *The Irish Times* (6 November 1996).

'For those in favour of retaining the ban, the issue is an emotive one which goes to the heart of all that has happened

over the past 30 years. They see the rule as a provision which defiantly reproaches the security forces of a state hostile to Irish culture. By so doing, they miss the point that Rule 21 is as much part of the sectarian landscape as a protest against it.'
Irish Times editorial (30 May 1998).

'The GAA could remove the ban on the security forces so opening the game up to one million Protestants who up to now have shied away from the sport.'
Trevor Ringland, former rugby international and Ulster Unionist supporter, in a letter to *The Irish Times* (11 June 1996).

'It's about time the GAA woke up. The ban has been gone since 1973 – if Frank Sinatra can play in Croke Park, then why not the Irish international rugby team?'
Pat Daly, Éire Óg delegate at the GAA convention in Cork.

'Will the GAA's Rule 21 apply to purchasers of its proposed computer game?'
Letter to *The Irish Times* (14 November 2003).

'Rule 21 lasted for almost a century but passed away quietly in just over an hour.'
Martin Breheny, *Irish Independent* (November 2001).

Christy:
One Ring to Rule Them All

Although we can't be certain Christy Ring was the greatest hurler of all time, folklore long ago made life easy for us by deciding that he was. The result is a cascade of wisdom – some about him, some from the man himself and some attributed to him for no good reason.

'You would hear people talking about the flukey goal that Ring got. But the flukey goal that Ring got was the ball everybody else assumed was going to go over the bar or go wide. From the time he went on the field, he never took his eyes off the ball.'

Austin Flynn of Waterford, quoted in Colm Keane, *Hurling's Top Twenty* (2002).

'Keep your eye on the ball, even when it's in the referee's pocket.'

Christy Ring, advice to aspiring hurlers.

'The hardest things that you must do in training will serve you well in the game, because you will never have to do them as hard again.'

Christy Ring, on training.

'Ah, Andy, I'm sorry I didn't do that to you an hour ago.'

Christy Ring, after splitting Waterford's Andy Fleming during a league match.

'By God Christy, we'll have to shoot you.'

Mick Rattler Byrne of Tipperary, after Christy scored the winning point in a league game against Tipperary. Christy replied, 'Oh sure ye might as well, Mickey, ye've tried everything else.'

'Stick a pen-knife in every football.'

Christy Ring, suggestion for the promotion of hurling.

'After mass, after school, in the morning, in the evening, after matches.'

Christy Ring, on training.

'When I know all about it, then I'll give it up.'

Christy Ring (attrib.), quoted in Brendan Fullam, *Hurling Giants* (1994).

'The funny thing about Christy Ring is the older he got the better he got. He was better in his latter years than when he started.'

John Doyle, quoted in Colm Keane, *A Cut Above the Rest* (1999).

'If he [the playwright] had not been a Glenman, I would have walked out.'

Christy Ring, on seeing Val Dorgan's play, *The Hurler*.

'Christy was very sharp, accurate, tense. He was a great hurler and a match winner. Mick was more even as a person. He didn't get too excited about it before or after. He was a different kind of character. You couldn't compare the two of them at all.'

Dick Stokes of Limerick, team-mate of Mick Mackey, on the great Ring vs Mackey question, quoted in Colm Keane, *Hurling's Top Twenty* (2002).

'We're the best in everything now.'

Christy Ring, on winning the county double with Glen Rovers and St Nicholas (1954).

'When you pass a centre-back, you're heading straight for goal, but when you come in from the wing, you have the centre-forward and corner-back to beat.'

Christy Ring, on playing wing half-forward (his least favourite position).

'In hurling, you hit the ball and it is a goal, or a point, or a wide, and maybe once in a while it comes back to you. In squash, it just keeps coming back.'

Christy Ring, on squash (another sport at which he excelled).

'I don't want to be recognised.'

Christy Ring, when asked why he put a cap on before a match.

'Never put frills on the first ball, always get rid of it.'

Christy Ring to Phil Shanahan, quoted in Brendan Fullam, *Legends of the Ash* (1997).

'Maybe none of us in Blackpool gave enough thought to Cloyne. They had just loaned Ring to us. Now that he was back it was to Cloyne that hurling followers would come to remember him.'

Val Dorgan, in his biography of Christy.

'You probably think I am a respected man in this town. There are people in this town, boy, that think I am locked up the red house on the hill all week and only let out to hurl on Sunday.'

Christy Ring, quoted in Breandán Ó hEithir, *Over the Bar* (1984).

'No one.'

Christy Ring, when asked who was marking him in the final 10 minutes of the 1956 match against Limerick in which time he scored 3 goals for a Cork victory.

'The Christy Ring whose memory I perpetuate in bronze will be the perfect athlete that he was in his youth, strong, but elegant like Apollo of Greek mythology of Michelangelo's *David*, men never marked by the passage of time.'

Yann Goulet, sculptor.

'Who was the hardest man to play on? The man who wouldn't play the ball.'

Christy Ring (attrib.).

'One legend is that he honed his accuracy by shooting a ball from 20 yards at the bell button on the parish priest's door. Another was that he used to lob a ball into a bucket hanging from a tree 30 or 40 yards away.'

Denis Walsh (29 February 2004).

'Sure I didn't see Jesus Christ either and everyone knows he was the greatest!'

Dr Jim Young, Cork hurler, when asked how he knew that Ring was the greatest when he had never seen him play.

'He must have the greatest hurling brain of all who ever caught a stick. This would have been a match rather than a massacre but for Ring.'

John D. Hickey, on the 1959 Railway Cup final, *Irish Independent*. Christy scored 4–5 of Munster's 7–11, 5 points more than Connacht's total of 2–6.

'He was like a ballet dancer. He'd just pull and turn in the one movement and maybe score a point.'

Billy Rackard of Wexford.

'Even though he was fairly lucid when he was playing he had this bit of hurling madness that brought him out of the ordinary hurler's sphere.'

Jimmy Smyth of Clare, quoted in Colm Keane, *Hurling's Top Twenty* (2002).

'Ring would be remembered if he had never won anything. His enormous incomparable skill must stand as his monument.'

Paddy Downey.

'He developed the under-21 free taking style we see other people using now. He would lift and move the ball in a bit before getting the full power behind it. He succeeded in perfecting that and he got goal after goal by using it.'

Con Murphy, team-mate, quoted in Colm Keane, *Hurling's Top Twenty* (2002).

'As long as the red jerseys of Cork and the blue of Munster and the green, black and gold of Glen Rovers, colours that Christy wore with such distinction, as long as we see these colours in manly combat the memories of Christy's genius and prowess will come tumbling back with profusion.'

Jack Lynch, speaking at Christy's funeral.

'It's a mortal sin to bury a man like him.'

Woman, speaking at Christy's funeral.

'He could make a ball talk.'

Jimmy Doyle of Tipperary.

'How oft I've watched him from the Hill, move here and there in grace/In Cork, Killarney, Thurles Town or by the Shannon's race/Now Cork is bet the hay is saved, the thousands wildly sing/They speak too soon, my sweet garsún, for here comes Christy Ring.'

Bryan MacMahon, 'Ballad of Christy Ring'.

Clubs and Clubmen

The building blocks of the GAA are the 2,000-odd clubs that anchor the association in the heart of the communities of Ireland. Even the most modest of them has a mythology, a history and a cast of characters relating to victories, incidents and matches of the recent and not-so-recent past. The greatest inter-county players come back to play for their clubs the week after their exploits are televised to more than half a million people. For most of the year, the clubs and their army of volunteers toil away in the background, but every St Patrick's Day, the four best get to play the All-Ireland final in Croke Park – but in a way, they are all there every year.

'No soccer team has a name quite as lovely as that belonging to Fighting Cocks of Carlow.'
Weblog, 101 reasons why the GAA is better than soccer.

'Give any half-decent clubman a choice between his club winning the junior championship and his county winning an All-Ireland and it is no contest. The club win every time and rightly so – every savage should love his native shore. When you play for a team the greatest satisfaction comes from watching the diverse talents of farmer, teacher, banker, businessman and student being as one in the pursuit of some crazy goal.'

Colm O'Rourke, *Sunday Independent* (23 November 2003).

'Any word of the Dreadnoughts, Seán? Will they ever take on the Man-O-War?'

Seán Óg Ó Ceallacháin, referee, quoting supporters' reaction to his Sunday-night club result broadcasts.

'Clogherhead Dreadnoughts, the only club banned for life from playing GAA. Twice.'

Breandán Ó hEithir, *Sunday Tribune* (1982).

'The GAA club and all the people who do things there because they just love doing them became the answer to the sugar-coated fascism of a modern world which presumes to know what's best for everyone.'

Tom Humphries, *The Irish Times* (14 April 2003).

'The club treasurer spends some time at the AGM lamenting the yearly cost of running a club and especially the bill for hurleys; a month later, the team is being urged to give 'em timber lads – we have plenty of hurleys on the sideline.'

Weblog, The O'Byrne Files.

'This spine of Irishness consists of thousands of people voluntarily spending hundreds of thousands of hours a year coaching young people and working for their local clubs, all because they love their sport, the good it does for their communities, and the good it does Ireland. It is that sense of locale which gives GAA its very rootedness in Irish life.'

Kevin Myers, *The Irish Times* (25 August 2004).

'I never retired. They just stopped picking me.'

Tony Scullion, Derry full-back, explaining the manner of his departure from the inter-county game.

'The directions from Swatragh were accurate enough. Turn left, then right until you know you are really lost. Then look to your left and you can't miss the GAA field.'

Jack Boothman, former GAA president.

'I never followed the Glen when I was growing up, but there was something mystical and magical about the name. You hear people talking about the spirit of the Glen and it's all true.'

Seánie McGrath.

'An occasion which the GAA's founders would have treasured. The inhabitants of a small, rural parish on the shores of Lough Neagh relocated to the birthplace of the Association for St Patrick's Day to watch their heroes carve their own special niche in football history.'

Martin Breheny, *Irish Independent* (2002). Ballinderry, a club from an area with just 300 households, won the 2002 club football championship.

'At a recent meeting of South Dublin GAA leagues, I was astounded to hear than one of the great historical clubs of the capital city could neither get enough players nor mentors to keep a team in the league.'

P.J. Cunningham, *Irish Independent* (23 November 2000).

'Apart from money for inter-county players, the biggest hot potato in the GAA currently is the state of club fixtures in many, but not all, counties. Competitions starting in the spring and not being finished until Christmas. Or a first round county championship game in April and the next round not taking place until three months later because of club players being involved with the county team. That is why in many counties the two busiest months of the year for club fixtures are November and December and the slackest months are June, July and August.'

Eugene McGee (10 November 2003).

'It was decided to take only one car for those who had no bicycles and the rest of the team to cycle.'

Minutes of Ballyskenagh meeting, detailing transport arrangements for match in Moneygall (15 June 1949), quoted by Chris Dooley, *The Irish Times* (4 October 2003).

'The difference between winning a club and a county All-Ireland is when you get a slap on the back after the club match, you actually know the person when you turn around.'

Tomas Meehan of Caltra, after winning the 2004 football club final.

Commitment

For an amateur game, the GAA demands a great deal of pre-match preparation. Until the 1950s, two-week training 'camps' were used by teams to prepare for big matches, but this smacked too much of professionalism and was outlawed. Three-times-a-week gatherings were normal until the 1970s, when Dublin and Kerry upped the training regimes to five times a week. Ger Loughnane's legendary training sessions with Clare in the 1990s raised the bar even higher or, to be more precise, earlier, with early-morning sessions for the hurling team that was rewarded with All-Ireland titles in 1995 and 1997. There have been deviations from the trend, most notably Mickey Harte's less intensive programme for the 2003 Tyrone All-Ireland winning team, but training, and its toll on people, remains one of the major topics of conversation among GAA people.

'Paddy Bawn's idea of preparation of a game was a day ashore to recover his land legs.'
Con Houlihan.

'Many modern parents regard underage GAA activity as a free child-minding service.'

Eugene McGee, *Irish Independent* (19 January 2004).

'I have heard every excuse for being late for training. The best of all was the player who told me he was late because the wheel fell off his mobile home.'

Eugene McGee, Offaly manager.

'We're taking this match awful seriously. We're training three times a week now, and some of the boys are off the beer since Tuesday.'

Weblog.

'None. But I was out threshing until ten o'clock every night. What training would I need?'

Paddy Martin of Kildare, when asked what training he had done for the 1928 All-Ireland.

'We went to college but we would have had no interest in books, we only went to university to play football.'

Cathal O'Rourke of Armagh.

'In certain minds, it's always chains and ashes. Especially in places like Wexford and Clare. "Jaysus, boy, we dragged tractors through bogs." It's a load of nonsense. You couldn't win an All-Ireland doing that.'

Liam Griffin, Wexford hurling manager.

'The main thing is, they'd eat grass to win. That's what I want. I'm not interested in lads ringing me up saying that they can't train because they need a babysitter, or their mother is not well, or there's someone after passing away.'

Larry Tompkins, Cork manager, revealing the calibre of player best suited to his laid-back style or management.

'When I joined the Cavan panel in 1992, I became conditioned to going from Dublin to Cavan for training, never being able to plan a weekend away, always feeling like a convict if I had a pint on the Saturday night before a game (every Saturday is the night before a game).'

Paul O'Dowd, Cavan goalkeeper.

'Eventually the body can't take any more. Chronic overload. There's no doubt that long-term injuries are on the increase, absolutely none, as a result of the repetitive stress on bones, muscles, ligaments and tendons. We're imposing tremendous strain on young players who aren't ready for it, and we're making it worse by not giving them sufficient time to recover.'

Dr Niall Moyna, DCU coach and a senior lecturer in exercise physiology.

'The GAA should thank its lucky stars that someone doesn't take them to court. I mean the European Court of Human Rights'

All-Ireland hurling manager on the increased intensity of training, quoted by Vincent Hogan, *Irish Independent.*

'If two poor teams are on a pitch and one is much fitter that team will win.'

Kevin Heffernan.

'Just as there are racehorses that cannot cope with soft ground, so there are footballers that feel ill suited to early-season training. Hard ground specialists consider the dedicated winter trainers to be mere point-to-pointers, whereas they are the genuine flat-race thoroughbred. With the recent good weather, they will have started to appear at training sessions throughout the country in their droves.'

Weblog, The O'Byrne Files.

'There were times when we only had one sliotar so if it got lost we would become one big search party.'

Noel Skehan of Kilkenny.

'Will impress for twenty minutes before pulling a muscle and signalling wildly to the line that they need replacing.'

Weblog, The Typical Junior Team.

'I am not too sure whether injuries today are all for real or some might be in players' heads. I believe the reason we have so many injuries in modern-day football is that players are playing from January to December. That's a major problem and I don't know of any other organisation in the world that does that.'

Mick O'Dwyer, speaking on Radio Kerry (December 2000).

'The GAA is a great organisation for awards, from man-of-the-match prizes in under-10 games all the way up to the pinnacle of the business, an All Star award and the chance to meet Marty Morrissey. In fact, there are so many awards available to GAA players that you would want to be a really poor player not to collect enough trophies to line your mantelpiece during your career, no matter what level you compete at. And even if you can't kick a ball or swing a hurley, you can still pick up an award for Club Person of the Year or Supporter of the Year.

Eugene McGee, *Irish Independent* (19 January 2004).

'The only time in my playing days I heard anybody talking about hamstrings was when they were hanging outside a butcher's shop.'

Mick Rattler Byrne of Tipperary.

'I wouldn't know what to do with a hamstring injury, probably ate it.'

Louth footballer (1957).

'Hamstring injuries were there and probably weren't recognised. Although players are running faster now than before, which does put more strain on the hamstring.'

Dr Con Murphy, Cork team doctor.

'I was stood many a drink by GAA enthusiasts.'

Paddy Kehoe, explaining how his weight rocketed to 16 stone 10lbs, quoted in Brendan Fullam, *Legends of the Ash* (1997).

'The day we quit hurling is the day we all become 40 stone.'

Setanta Ó hAilpín.

Croke Park and Its Doors

Mr Butterly's recreational ground became GAA property in 1910 and has been at the heart of the association ever since. Throughout history, it has reflected the aspirations of GAA followers and others. The modest pavilion of 1910; the rubble from the Easter Rebellion used to construct Hill 16; the grey corrugated stands of the teens; the peculiarly sectioned Hogan Stand of 1924; the pillioned Cusack Stand of 1938; the cantilevered Hogan Stand of 1959; and the redeveloped triple decker of 1996, designed by Gilroy MacMahon – all were amongst Dublin's most important construction projects of their era. No wonder they have been picky about allowing their rivals in.

'Taj Ó Maolmhichíl.'
Sunday Business Post headline, on the reconstructed Croke Park (1999).

'If you look behind the goals at the moment, goalkeepers have very little room to go back and kick-out the ball. I think the situation is crazy as the whole system is governed towards trying to get people into the stadium while forgetting about the players and the game.'

Mick O'Dwyer, speaking on Radio Kerry (December 2000).

'As you get older you realise what you're walking in to and you get even more nervous.'

John Doyle, Tipperary hurler, quoted in Colm Keane, *A Cut Above the Rest* (1999).

'Another ding-dong battle in Jones' Road, but this one was a little different. A struggle for people's attention, between venue and event.

Diarmuid Murphy, on the opening of the third phase of the Croke Park redevelopment, *Irish Examiner*.

'The echoes of surround sound finally faded in Croke Park.'

Seán Moran, *The Irish Times*.

'The ground at Jones' Road is altogether unsuited for hurling and the game was to a certain extent spoiled for its rough surface.'

P.P. Sutton, sports correspondent (1895).

'Who wants to win an All-Ireland in a building site anyway?'

Graham Geraghty, the Meath captain, after his county were eliminated form the 1998 Leinster championship.

'The old Croke Park looked like it was dreamt up by Bram Stoker, all shadows and cobwebs and crepuscular faces peering out from narrow boxes as they pocketed your money.

Even on scorching days, children under 12 walked around the place with blue lips. Men whose idea of a pleasurable afternoon was a good bout of bare-knuckle fighting trembled at the thought of visiting the jacks. The old stadium felt like it was set in frost and that was fine because thousands came on the principle that they would be warmed by the game.'

Keith Duggan, *The Irish Times* (9 August 2003).

'The more used you get to playing Croke Park the worse it gets.'

Páidí Ó Sé, quoted in Colm Keane, *A Cut Above the Rest* (1999).

'They must have got the plans out in California. I mean, the climate in Ireland is one of plenty wind and rain and if you go and sit at front of the new stand where the Cusack once was, you will get drenched. I have seen people running to get from the front to the back. If you were to design a house in a similar fashion, where the wind blew into your sitting room while you watched *Coronation Street*, you would nearly be certified.'

Mick O'Dwyer, speaking on Radio Kerry (December 2000).

'The GAA, by and large, keeps Croke Park for itself and for the games it promotes. Only in such an insecure, self-hating culture as ours could this be considered a crime, but there you go.'

Tom Humphries, *The Irish Times* (14 April 2003).

'GAA, its work amongst its own supporters has been socially of the greatest value and the redevelopment of Croke Park

was a brave undertaking at a time when there were no plans for national stadiums on the public agenda.'
Irish Times editorial (9 April 2001).

'It's not as if the GAA is being asked to sell the family silver; merely rent it at the going rate.'
Letter to The Irish Times (10 April 2001).

'I regard the GAA as being deficient and immoral in its introduction of Saturday fixtures, which represent sheer larceny of local residents' free time.'
Letter to The Irish Times (17 August 2001).

'We are becoming an organisation which facilitates everything and stands for nothing.'
Con Murphy, former GAA president, on the opening of Croke Park to soccer (16 April 2005).

'Croak Park.'
Dublin colloquialism for Glasnevin Cemetery, the city's largest graveyard within sight of Croke Park.

'A useful discussion of how the biggest professional sport in the world has no stadium for itself becomes an attack on an amateur, sports/cultural organisation which won't kow-tow.'
Tom Humphries, The Irish Times (14 April 2003).

'For most of the big changes in the GAA in recent years the catalyst has been money. GAA officers used to claim they would never allow sponsorship. They did for the money. They claimed we would never see the name of an alcoholic drink company attached to a GAA competition. We did for the money. They claimed that we would never see "foreign games" played in Croke Park. We will for the money.'

Eugene McGee (18 August 2003).

'The fact of the matter is that the GAA has given far more to the Exchequer than it has received – by way of taxes that have accrued as a result of its investment in Croke Park and other grounds throughout the country, not to mention the employment and revenue generated by its activities. It has also made an inestimable contribution to the mental and physical health of the nation through its provision of facilities and its voluntary promotion of games and pastimes, particularly among the young..'

Danny Lynch, GAA PRO (8 October 2004).

'Why would the GAA, after having gone to enormous lengths to build a world-class stadium, solve the problems of other sporting bodies?'

Letter to *The Irish Times* (13 December 2003).

'If you believe soccer, rugby, Gaelic football, ladies' football and camogie and others sports can all be played on the same pitch then you have to be a bit of a nitwit.'

Bertie Ahern.

'When we see the shamefully obvious political act of awarding £20 million to the already overflowing coffers of the GAA (bolstered by embarrassingly engineered draws and subsequent fruitful replays), we have to ask ourselves: is this all we can expect? Is this all we can attain? Is watching these undisciplined players, whose skill seems to be secondary only to unrestrained violence on the pitch, and with all its attendant influences on our young people, the height of our sports culture? It must be soul destroying to feel deserted by one's country, especially in favour of insular amateurism and inter-county tribalism.'

Letter to *The Irish Times* (29 July 1998).

'Hill 16 has a unique atmosphere unmatched at any other sporting venue in Ireland. For this reason alone, its existence must be preserved.'

Letter to *The Irish Times* (31 May 1999).

'The stadium it has built is the best and most confident answer Michael Hogan's tribe could ever have given to Bloody Sunday.'

Tom Humphries, *The Irish Times* (5 January 2004).

'Given the largesse already shown by Burlington Bertie to the Football Association of Ireland, the GAA was entitled to around IR£60 million in government assistance whether they opened up Croke Park or not.'

Liam Cahill, An Fear Rua website (April 2001).

'The GAA got £20 million because it is a unique and thriving sporting and cultural organisation, providing healthy recreation in every corner of the country. It got £20 million because it is the only sporting organisation with an advanced plan for a 21st century facility on the table. It got £20 million because after a decade of governmental pillaging of lottery sports funding, £20 million is the least our premier sports body deserves. It got £20 million because it is an extra-ordinary community-based amateur organisation competing against some of the world's great professional sports. Most of all, it got £20 million because at last as a nation, riding along on the back of the big fat eternally smug Celtic Tiger, we are beginning to appreciate that sport is a resource worthy of investment and care. Sport is not a luxury; it is a part of our lives which impinges on health, education and welfare.'

Tom Humphries, *The Irish Times* (5 December 1997).

'The proposals that the goalkeeper can tee his kick-out and that a player can now lift the ball directly from the ground are a disgrace. There will be no point in opening up Croke Park, as the way this is going soccer will be played there soon anyway.'

Letter to *The Irish Times* (16 December 2004).

'They got the planning permission for a structure of that scale simply because of who they are. The attitude of the Croke Park administrators towards the local people has been beyond contempt. Really, they have refused to recognise the exist-ence of the locals.'

Tony Gregory TD, on Croke Park.

'I would not let anybody into the car park, not to mention into Croke Park.'

Dan Hoare, treasurer of Munster Council.

'I fail to see how allowing a sport where its Northern fans hound out their Catholic players, whilst their Southern fans see no problem booing a Danish player and a Georgian player simply for playing with a Scottish club of Protestant heritage will help banish any perceived sectarianism from Croke Park.'

Letter to *The Irish Times* (13 December 2003).

'Spare a thought for the Croke Park residents, who unaccustomed to our ways didn't notice a big stadium beside their house when they moved in...They are still awaiting a reply to the stern letter they sent to the Black and Tans regarding the dreadful racket on Bloody Sunday.'

Tom Humphries, *The Irish Times* (24 September 2001).

'The people of Ireland only contributed about 10 per cent of the construction costs of the stadium and the rest was funded from the GAA's own resources. Such being the case, nobody is going to be able to force the GAA to make the ground available to anyone.'

Letter to *The Irish Times* (30 June 2003).

'Thanks to the infamous £20 million, we are responsible for every ailment that afflicts Irish society. From drug abuse to facilities for the disabled, from the homeless to the aged, from childcare to the state of non-national roads, we are now to blame. This accursed £20 million. Over the next three years the government will spend £50 billion in the current account. This can now be broken into two lots: the £20 million the GAA will get and the £49,980 million the GAA won't get. Of the two, the former is clearly the most valuable. The first £20 million can cure all the ills of Irish life. It has the miraculous ability to expand to meet the needs of every pressure group in the country. For the next 50 years every complaint about a funding shortfall from every organisation in Ireland will be made with references to this £20 million. And we, the GAA, have it. It's quite obvious what we should do. We should give it back. Yes. We should give it back and get a completely different £20 million, a £20 million without all the curative, magical powers.'

Letter to *The Irish Times* (7 January 1998).

Divine Intervention

In an organisation where bishops, priests and clerical men serve as patrons in many areas, it is normal to expect that the Divine should take a hand in Gaelic affairs. Galway were, apparently, cursed by a priest in 1923, and it took them until 1980 to win another All-Ireland. You can't be too careful.

'God, he was a great minor.'
Breandán Ó hEithir, *Sunday Tribune* (1982).

'We would rather beat Kilkenny fair.'
Eudie Coughlan of Cork, when told that the mass on All-Ireland Sunday morning was being offered up for victory. According to Brendan Fullam's *Hurling Giants* (1994), Coughlan offered a note of thanks in the Sacred Heart messenger after Cork won (1926).

'From the beginning to the end of the match, I did not hear a single syllable that the purest minded boy or girl on the face

of God's earth would not listen to. The same cannot be said of other games played that were played in the metropolis.'
Fr John Gwynne SJ, on the 1913 Croke Cup final.

'My innocent childhood perception of the priesthood changed after that game.'
Sambo McNaughton on marking Iggy Clarke of Galway.

'One of the biggest memories I would have from the game was the ref trying to keep the crowd off the field. Tom Dempsey was appealing to the crowd to stay off the field. It was running through my mind that God if the crowd don't keep off the field the game will be called off. Imagine that running through your head. I suppose it shows how much bad luck we had over the years. Even when we were eight points up there was still a fear somewhere in my mind that the game could be taken off us. In all the years that I had been hurling for Wexford the man above wasn't on our side. He wasn't even giving us a fair chance, he didn't even give us 50–50.'
Martin Storey, Wexford hurler from the 1980s and 1990s.

'We have seen great crowds stand to attention whilst "Faith of Our Fathers" echoed around the field, and we shall never forget the scene when the Angelus bell rang out – the ball was forgotten, and the hurleys lay idle, whilst players and spectators joined in silent prayers of homage.'
J.M. Hayes of Tipperary, a GAA historian.

Down Under

One of the great mysteries of football is how the Australian and Irish codes managed to get together a successful international series with big crowds and a bigger television audience. One uses an oval ball and the other a round ball, after all. Although that could have been an advantage...

'This international rules series was a bit like the Vietnam War. Nobody at home cared about it, but everyone involved sure did.'

Leigh Matthews, the Australian coach.

'The lesson in sporting sociology began early, the Australian party's bus, given a police escort if you don't mind (for a few the first in which they had been willing participants), weaving down the narrow, terraced streets towards the historic stadium to be greeted by thousands of fans walking the same way.'

Rohan Connolly of realfooty.com.au, on the 2000 All-Ireland final.

'If under-17 footballers from Ireland succeeded with the Australian ball and managed to win the series, I don't see why senior players cannot do the same.'
Vincent Banville, in a letter to *The Irish Times* (19 October 1999).

'You have to catch them first.'
Australian player, when asked why he hadn't flattened more opponents.

'The Final Quarter Pounders.'
Irish Sun headline, on Australia–Ireland international rules match (2001).

'To the sound of a didgeridoo a lone warrior covered from head-to-toe in war paint raced to the halfway line carrying the aboriginal flag. The streaker at the Leinster final was wearing more. God, aren't the GAA getting very liberal?'
Kieran Cunningham, *The Star*.

'The fools. The fools. They know not what they've done. By performing such heroics in Australia, the Irish "Irrational Rules" team have unwittingly put forward a compelling case for the immediate abolition of this nation's most popular sport, Gaelic football.'
Kevin O'Shaughnessy, *Irish Independent* (18th October 1999).

Drink:
The Demon of Discord

The construction of social clubs throughout the country, and the advent of commercial sponsorship, led the GAA into a quandary it has not quite tackled – how to balance its role in promoting healthy pursuits with the profoundly ambivalent pursuit of drinking alcohol. The jury is still out.

'Drinking won't end when we have the Eat Your Greens All-Ireland Hurling Championship.'
Tom Humphries, *The Irish Times* (10 March 2003).

'Drill holes in the GAA cups to prevent drinking.'
John Vaughan, Tipperary board delegate.

'A match at football between the villages in this neighbourhood has been attended with effects particularly distressing. The lads met on the green at Ballitore, from whence, when the sport was over, they, with many of the spectators, adjourned to this place in perfect good humour; but the demon of discord, whiskey, soon introduced a battle in which all were engaged and almost all suffered. A man who had for some time made a desperate fight was at length brought to the ground by the stroke of a bottle from the wife of a person whom he had just knocked down; and the woman's feelings for her husband being stimulated by liquor, she cut the head of his opponent to innumerable pieces, and immediately received from one of the combatants a casual blow that fractured her own. There is little prospect of her recovery. Two men in prison in Athy are likewise despaired of, and a multitude of others are dangerously wounded. Ill fares the land where the industry, morals, health and even lives of the lower orders in its inhabitants are sacrificed to revenue; and ill must it ever fare whilst the vitals of the country are sacrificed to support the Government.'

The Observer (November 1792).

'The GAA – a haven of drunkenness and injury.'

Diarmuid Ferriter, historian, *Ireland Transformed* (2004).

'The GAA's claim that it does great work for the youth of this country is somewhat negated by its selling out to Guinness.'

Letter to *The Irish Times* (4 January 2001).

'Sport is not a goody-goody, squeaky clean, all-sins-absolved-while-you-wait deal. It's part of mainstream community life. Like drink is... The GAA should ignore all the sententious cavilling about the Guinness sponsorship of hurling. Not a whelp last week about Le Heineken Cup. Not a breezy swing of the crozier over Witness. Not a whimper about

Celtic's Carling shirts. Not a moan about quality TV shows like *The Sopranos* being sponsored by Miller. Not a question about pols (from the Taoiseach down) opening pubs seven days a week. Guinness have been good for hurling and vice versa. Get over it. The wider culture is the problem.'

Tom Humphries, *The Irish Times* (10 March 2003).

'How did Ireland's premier sporting organisation come to own the largest chain of licensed premises in the country, with more than 100 outlets and a group turnover estimated at □190 million?'

Letter to *The Irish Times* (17 July 2004).

'The GAA rid itself of tobacco money, partly due to the medical outcry, yet the rising drink culture has yet to dawn on associations whose lifeblood is youth, and who are insidiously "introduced" to the tipple through sport. Far be it from me to outlaw something I too enjoy, but any association or group which has youth at its core cannot brandish such advertising before their gullible eyes and not expect a proportion of them not to "take" that road, if only though peer pressure.'

Paul Donaghy, sportswriter, *Carlow Nationalist*.

'I wonder what my fellow Clareman Micheál Ó Ciosog would say about it? I can only imagine him turning in his grave at the sight of the porter peddler's name hanging off the McCarthy Cup.'

Letter to *The Irish Times* (6 September 2000).

Early Days

There are not many modern sporting organisations that have paid as much attention to the rhetoric of their formative years as the GAA. The debate about the GAA was not really about athletics, hurling and football at all, but between national and imperial values, the colonial ascendancy and the ordinary people who wanted a bit of recreation on their day off. It got hot and heavy and, unfortunately, for many GAA officials it remained hot and heavy after the rest of the country stopped being concerned with such matters.

'The three men with whom the founding of the GAA has been traditionally associated had much in common, but it may be said that Cusack represented the Gaelic ideal, Davin the athletic and Archbishop Croke the disciplinary ideal.'
Seán Ó Siochain, GAA secretary, in a report to Congress (1952).

'The old game of hurling has fallen so completely into oblivion that those appointed to procure hurls and balls discovered that the art of manufacturing these articles was as extinct as the dodo. This difficulty is being got over, and early next week old Irish hurls will be on sale once more.'

Michael Cusack, *Irish Sportsman* (1882).

'No movement having for its object the social and political advancement of a nation from the tyranny of imported and enforced customs and manners can be regarded as perfect if it has not made adequate provision for the preservation and cultivation of the national pastimes of the people.

'We tell the Irish people to take the management of their games into their own hands, to encourage and promote in every way every form of athletics which is peculiarly Irish, and to remove with one sweep everything foreign and iniquitous in the present system.

'The vast majority of the best athletes in Ireland are nationalists. These gentlemen should take the matter in hands at once, and draft laws for the guidance of the promoters of meetings in Ireland next year.

'The people pay the expenses of the meetings, and the representatives of the people should have the controlling power. It is only by such an arrangement that pure Irish athletics will be revived, and the incomparable strength and physique of our race will be preserved.'

Michael Cusack, *United Ireland*, the Land League newspaper (11 October 1884).

'Michael Cusack has set up the Dublin Hurling Club for the purposes of taking steps to re-establish the national game of hurling. So far as is practicable rules shall be framed to make a transition from hurley to hurling as easy as the superiority of the latter game will permit.'

Irish Sportsman (1882).

'To test the pulse of the nation, a hurling club was established in Dublin.'

Michael Cusack, *United Ireland*, the Land League newspaper (3 January 1885).

'Some years ago people in Dublin were giving our national game the exceedingly diminutive name of hurley. I warned them that if they did not adhere to the form in which I introduced it, I would call cricket crickey, and then they stopped. Nobody plays hurley now in Dublin and I am told that very few play crickey anywhere in Ireland.'

Michael Cusack, *The Celtic Times* (3 September 1887).

'For some months back we have been hearing a good deal of a movement which has been on foot for reviving the almost extinct Irish game of hurling. We were under the impression that the game in its true form was so fearfully dangerous and so productive of troublesome feelings that no sane man would attempt to revive it. We were extremely glad to see it demonstrated week after week in the Phoenix Park by Mr Cusack and the students attending his academy that the dan-gers existed only in the imagination of nervous people who either disliked the game or knew nothing about it.'

Irish Sportsman (Easter 1884).

'If a hurling club or a cricket club was got up with its regular place and hour of meeting, and mixing of amusement and politics which would be an additional attraction it could serve also as a Confederate Club of the Young Ireland movement.'

The Nation (24 June 1848).

"The English game of cricket is very much in vogue in Ireland. It has completely displaced the old athletic exercise of hurling so prevalent some years ago.'

Nenagh Guardian (20 June 1873).

'In clubs in Dublin frequented by Catholics and Protestants, skittles and rackets are played on Sundays. The skittle-alley and the racket court are open to rich people, but the fields of Ireland are not to be opened to the people of Ireland the same day. This impudent absurdity will be removed by the GAA.'

Michael Cusack, *United Ireland,* the Land League newspaper (14 March 1885).

'If we see that the rising generation receives that athletic exercise and training which should co-exist with a bold and spirited people, and if we impress upon them the great necessity for vigorous and manly practices, we shall be doing great work for the preservation of the Irish race and the future glory of the Irish nation.'

Michael Cusack, in the oldest-surviving edition of *The Celtic Times* (19 February 1887).

'Games grow out of the soil, just as plants do. Hurling grew out of the soil of Ireland.'

Michael Cusack, *The Celtic Times* (26 February 1887).

'If I omitted representatives of the north east corner of Ireland, it is because the Dublin Athletic Club committee in June 1882, declined to admit mixed patronage.'

Michael Cusack, *The Celtic Times* (19 March 1887).

'Old men have forgotten the miseries of the Famine and had their youth renewed by the sights and sounds that were evoked by the thrilling music of the camán, the well directed stroke of the Cúl Báire, or the swift stride of the Gaelic forward in his pursuit of the ball to victory. Many dark days have dawned over our country.

'Sorrow and trouble have likewise made their way into the homes and hamlets of our people. It is certain that, in some places, these clouds would have been darker, and care would have eaten more deeply into the hearts of many, had it not been for the pastime and pleasure created in the revival of the Irish games by the Gaelic Athletic Association.'

Michael Davitt (1884).

'While sympathizing with the class of mechanics and the rural population who meet for athletic exercises on Sundays from inability to meet on other days the holding of athletic meetings on Sundays is detrimental to the interests of amateur athletics in Ireland.'

Val Dunbar, motion to ICAC, quoted in the *Irish Sportsman* (21 December 1878).

'I have learned that the rules under which the races and other events came off were those of the GAA. That great organisation has conferred many benefits upon the muscle and manhood of Ireland and, not the least among them, was that of teaching the young men of Ireland their own laws and their own games. In doing so, and in inculcating the minds of the athletes of Ireland the knowledge that they have Gaelic laws to govern their sports, a practical lesson has been given in Home Rule. If we can make our own laws with reference to our pastimes, we can make our own laws in more serious matters.'

Michael Davitt, speaking at a Trades Council Sports (August 1890).

'The whole business must be worked from Munster. Suppose we hold a meeting of delegates in some central place in Tipperary on the 1st of November next. Don't bother your head about Dublin. The place couldn't well be worse than it is.'

Michael Cusack to Maurice Davin (26 April 1884).

'Irish football is a great game and worth going a long way to see when played on a fairly laid out ground and under proper rules. Many old people say just hurling exceeded it as a trial of men. I would not care to see either game now as the rules stand at present. I may say there are no rules and therefore those games are often dangerous.'

Maurice Davin (13 October 1884).

'There is strong belief that Dublin Castle is using the Gaelic Association to spread secret societies thereby dividing Irish nationalism.'

Father Teevan CC, Cavan, letter to Cavan convention (4 November 1889), quoted in Dan Gallogly, *Cavan's Football Story* (1984).

'Our national pastimes, our grand athletic games, are dying and will inevitably cease to exist if we do not forthwith arrest this withering disease.'

Denis Holland, *Irishman* (22 October 1859).

'Nationalists of Dublin! Support not the would-be wreckers of the GAA! Down with dissension! Discountenance disunion! Down with the men who would disgrace the association that has for its patrons the tried, true, and illustrious Irishmen: Archbishop Croke, C.S. Parnell, Michael Davitt and John O'Leary.

'Who are those men who try to prove that Irishmen are not worthy of self-government? The Grocers' Assistants Sports Committee. Do not by your presence at their meeting commit an act of treason to Ireland. God Save Ireland.'

Banners at *Freeman's Journal* meeting, quoted in *The Irish Times* (11 July 1887).

'Maurice Davin's name was put forward in opposition, and a confused show of hands was taken. It was now growing dark; the air was most oppressive and warm some of the delegates were smoking, a few were disputing. The debris of what had been once the petty sessions clerk's desk was strewn about in front of the reporters. The show of hands proved indecisive. Fitzgerald proposed that supporters of each candidate pass out into the courtyard through separate doors to be counted. At first, only Davin's supporters' door was opened, and out they poured into the yard. Then, suddenly, it was shouted that only Bennett's supporters were to go outside. As the Davinites tried to get back into the Court House they found their way blocked and only a proportion of them were able to do so. The door was then locked, and those outside the building mainly Davinites, were counted as voting for Bennett, those inside for Davin. Despite protests the result was then declared as 316 for Bennett, 210 for Davin.'

Freeman's Journal (10 November 1887).

'Our games were in a most grievous condition until the brave and patriotic men who started the Gaelic Athletic Association took their revival in hand. The instantaneous and extraordinary success which attended their efforts fills me with great hope for Ireland's future. The Association's work has done more for Ireland than all the speeches of politicians for the past five years. Besides reviving our national sports, the GAA has also revived national memories, the names of its clubs perpetuating the memory of many great and good Irishmen.'

Douglas Hyde (November 1892).

'Better there was never a Gaelic Association than to have it the cause of fell disunion.'

E.P. Gill, speaking at a meeting of the County Tipperary town commission, *Tipperary Advocate* (19 December 1887).

'As far as I know, and I have been a patron for years, the Association is purely an athletic body and that alone.'

Archbishop Croke, replying to a GAA delegation (21 April 1895), quoted in *Cork Examiner* (22 April 1895).

Fans and Fanblogs

Being a GAA fan is not something you sign up for. You get it by osmosis. You are born into a community, a county, a province – and rejecting your local club and county colours can become the equivalent of rejecting your birthright. It leads to certain crazy characteristics, which fans have opportunity to ventilate through a variety of burgeoning websites, blanket emails and weblogs. Much older, simpler and more effective is the overheard remark from the middle of a throng at a championship match. There are thousands of these witticisms the GAA could easily be renamed the Gaelic Aphorism Association, Cumann Leathscéil Gael. Below are just a few.

'A fan is someone who, if you have made an idiot of yourself on the pitch, doesn't think you've done a permanent job.'
Jack Lynch.

'In GAA you are not allowed to change counties. It's not like soccer where you can jump on a bandwagon and say vague things like, "I've always supported them, even when they weren't winning anything." (Indeed, "weemin" have been known to support a soccer team on the basis of fancying the French midfielder. Can't imagine that happening in the GAA.) County allegiance defies such logic. You can't support them unless you were born there.'

Pól Ó Múirí, *The Irish Times* (15 November 1999).

'We'd rather, I think, be in the cold and driving rain, freezing in our anoraks, in the middle of nowhere watching a meaningless challenge match. Roscommon versus Longford. Because, ah yes, then you know you're living!'

Sheepstealers.com, Roscommon fans' website.

'No one will expect onlookers unduly to withhold their enthusiasm and ardour on the occasion of big matches, and Irish human nature seems to revel in a good shout, whether of triumph or reproach.'

Dick Fitzgerald, *How to Play Gaelic Football* (1914).

'Even the workhouse wall which used to be availed of in the past by visiting non-paying spectators who did not dread the brand of that institution so long as it saved them gate money.'

Freeman's Journal report on the 1898 All-Ireland football final in Tipperary.

'The only jacks they can't flush.'

Dublin banner at the 1974 All-Ireland final.

'Páirc: the GAA fans Subbuteo. I remember on *Anything Goes* Pat Delaney and a Galway hurler (John Connolly I'm almost sure) played a demonstration game. The Galway fella was winning by a goal and a point to nil when the credits rolled, I firmly believe that that was a defining moment in Galway hurling in the '80s.'

Liam Cahill, An Fear Rua website.

'No one can blame a schoolboy or a street urchin for climbing a wall to see a game, but it was truly galling and humiliating to see the number of respectable looking men who adopted this means.'

P.P. Sutton, at Clonturk Park (1894).

'Fight for victory and victory is yours. If you don't win, I'll shoot the whole lot of you.'

Letter to Jim Smith, Cavan captain, before the 1935 All-Ireland final. Cavan won.

'Good hurling games are like sex films. They relieve frustration and tension.'

Joe Lynch.

'Being lifted over the turnstile was how nearly every kid my generation first saw Croke Park. Many of the top players in the country remember it this way.'

Frank Shouldice, *The Irish Times* (2 August 2003).

'All kinds of predictions will be heard before the first championship ball is even thrown in: Two teams whose names begin with the letter *M* will contest the All-Ireland final... If the swallows are flying low, it's a sure sign of bad weather and an even worse Connacht football final (fair enough, this one has a 99 per cent accuracy rate)... If the grass is still bare in

June, silage crops will be low, but a man with a hairy chest will be the winning All-Ireland captain (93 per cent accuracy rate).'

Sheepstealers.com, Roscommon fans' website.

'The club that has the greatest following usually gets there in this arena.'

P.P. Sutton, describing the atmosphere in the GAA's first north Dublin stadium, Clonturk Park (1895).

'The loudest cheer of the day from Tipperary fans is upon the arrival of the first fans to the stadium who then proceed to take the tin foil off the sandwiches. This is an ancient territory marking ritual.'

Weblog, Tipperary supporters.

'The Dub is a homely creature and travels to the country only on those rare occasions when it is unavoidable. Thus it was inevitable that Saturday in Thurles would be enlivened by tales of Dubs who had turned back for home disheartened by traffic at places like Monasterevan, Kildare or Athy. RTÉ might as well hand their phone-in programmes over to the AA Roadwatch people today, because great and unassuagable will be the grief of the Dub who left his burrow sometime after 10, picked up his mates, drove around looking for the right motorway and then found it choked with other Dubs.'

Tom Humphries, *The Irish Times*.

'Donegal to send Orangemen home in time for the 12th.'

Banner at the 2003 All-Ireland semi-final.

'The Dergvate, Gay Prior's pub, Tommy Tubridy's, The Bradog, The Drovers, MacGleogan's, The Pound Bar, Mc Sweeney's.'

Weblog, 101 reasons why the GAA is better than soccer.

'I travelled from Cork to Rosslare. Imagine my surprise and delight to find that almost the entire route especially between the towns of Youghal and New Ross was gloriously festooned with the blue and white colours of Greece! Such overwhelming support of one small country for another brought tears of joy to my eyes.'

Manolis Andropoulos from Athens, in a letter to *The Irish Times*.

'As you pull on your county colours, you carry with you everything your club stands for, and carry with you the hopes and dreams of those not fortunate to be selected.'

Letter to *The Irish Times*.

'Kerry for the jokes, Offaly for the Sam Maguire.'

Offaly banner at 1982 All-Ireland final.

'It is impossible to get people to work on a Sunday.'

Iarnród Éireann, responding to complaints about the rail service to the 1997 Munster final, quoted in *The Irish Times* (19 July 1997).

'We have had our wallets hoovered by the GAA, CIÉ and B&B fraternity and have, unwittingly, achieved a united, 31-county Ireland under the new ABC banner (Anyone But Clare). Even an ageing Offaly team seem to acquire the manic energy of a bull on Viagra at the sight of the saffron and blue. All of this, combined with the vagaries of Jimmy Cooney's watch, has left us Clare dragoons living on a diet of drip-feed Valium and anti-depressants. I appeal to the GAA that it makes an immediate submission to Brussels for Area Aid Support for the Clare supporters. Just enough to cover two meat teas in Mother Hubbard's, a night in a damp Drumcondra B&B and a ticket for the sheltered end of Hill 16. I suppose we were warned that it was never going to be easy.'

Letter to *The Irish Times* (28 August 1998).

'If you appear with a ticket, it's like appearing on a desert island with a McDonald's. They're all watching you. I wanted to leave a ticket in the hotel but yer man said no way. He said look at them out there, and there were about 200 eyes looking in at me, waiting for me to produce the ticket.'

Ger Loughnane.

'I mind the time I found an old neighbour very upset to see his cat scratching her claws on the bark of an old oak tree, the morning before a big match. "A sign of feckin rain. We're really fecked now. Our lads are feckin useless in the rain."'

Sheepstealers.com, Roscommon fans' website.

'Down to the Portobello for the beer, the crack, the beer, the women, the beer, the Sunday morning hangover, the beer, the oh sh**e what did to do with me ticket midday panic, the beer for 3 hours before the match, the oh will I sell me ticket and stay on the beer problem, the match, the oh sh**e I wish I didn't drink so much beer so as I wouldn't have gone to the jacks and missed that goal. The post-match beer, the sing-

song, the beer, the take the piss out of the losers, the beer, the
11pm drunk decision to go to Coppers, the beer, the sh**e
where are the taxis, the beer, the pick up a slapper nurse, the
beer, the Monday morning hangover and then back to
fecking work on Monday afternoon and have to face into
another 90 hours over the next 7 days.'

Fan's championship diary, quoted on a GAA website.

'It's not just about the players either. It's about the thousands
of would-be fans, like myself, who would love to attend
matches regularly from the month of April onwards but just
do not have the games to go to.'

Letter to *The Irish Times* (20 April 1999).

'To look into the faces of some of these boorish, barbarian
drunks is indeed a chilling experience. What I saw when I
tried to work out the mindset of these types was a gawky,
feckless bunch who obviously don't know the meaning of
restraint and who also have very deep-seated psychological
problems that need to be urgently tackled.'

Letter to *The Irish Times* (15 July 2003).

'Don't talk to me about Ballagh. That lot are stone mad. Mind
you it must be a great town to go drinking in when Ros take
on Mayo… So long as the hoors don't half kill each other.'

Sheepstealers.com, Roscommon fans' website.

'The drinking crew tend to be in their twenties or thirties and
they are very single. Often they don't turn up until half-time.
Sunday is not a good day for the crew. Attendance at the
match serves two vital functions. The first of these is to

establish what happened on the previous night. The second is to watch the match.'

Weblog, The GAA Supporter.

'It wasn't the Canaries, it was the seagulls.'

Man who put the holiday money on Dublin to win the 1975 All-Ireland and was forced to spend his holidays in Donabate rather than Tenerife, quoted in Con Houlihan, *The Back Page* (1998).

'Time was, not so very long ago for that matter, when hoteliers and restaurateurs looked forward to the month of September, to cater for the needs of all those Gaels drawn from every county in Ireland. Now, of course, the hotels are chock-full of spivs, drones and butterflies from the four corners of the globe, who are prepared to pay fancy prices for our succulent steaks and marvellous mixed grills and forget about the "charm of the native peasantry" or the wonderful sunsets of Connemara and Achill. But we would like to remind the get-rich quick merchants who, in the same breath, kow-tow and overcharge the erstwhile visitors, that tourists may come and tourists may go, but Croke Park will go on forever. The long view is the better view in the long run. In this respect, Dublin can learn a good deal from Thurles, where, on occasion of Munster hurling finals, no one goes home either hungry or thirsty.'

GAA Digest (August, 1948).

Fourth Estate:

Newspapers

An experienced GAA journalist once said that the GAA
don't read their coverage, they measure it. After an uncertain
start, the newspapers began to devote vast column inches to
GAA reports, previews and news. The characters who provided much of this material became as important in GAA
culture as those involved in organising and playing the games.
The tension between officials and player and the press and
the unique ceremonials and rituals devised by the GAA, particularly the dedicated press night, have acquired a folklore of
their own.

'Death of Hurling Immortal.'
Tipperary Star headline.

'The GAA pundit can get it wrong, spectacularly wrong,
entirely wrong, make an absolute hames of his predictions,
week after week and still, oh glory, still practise punditry.

Indeed, were the GAA pundit to have a proper job – like an accountant or teacher – they'd be given their cards by the end of the summer.'

Pól Ó Muirí, *The Irish Times* (16 August 2002).

'There were carrier pigeons released when the match was over to bring the news of who had won back to Cork.'

Dick Stokes, Limerick hurler from the 1930s, quoted in Colm Keane, *Hurling's Top Twenty* (2002).

'This season of mists and mellow mangel-wurzels is also the season when money, the magic mutagen, metamorphoses mundane managers into mayhap messiahs who very soon rejoin the myriad of messiahs manque.'

Kevin Cashman, *Sunday Independent* (October 2000).

'You'll find Peter Finnerty's estimation of the relative merits of Limerick and Wexford elsewhere on this page. I bet Peter goes for Limerick – and I bet he's wrong.'

Kevin Cashman, *Sunday Independent* (5 August 1993).

'The idiots in the newspaper are printing what the rats on the streets are telling them. Oi Mr Nationalist if you can't write any better than the episodes here in the last few weeks you should step back 'cos you're not able to report.'

Eddie Byrne, Carlow county board chairman (December 2004).

'Getting a one-on-one chat with Osama bin Laden would be less trouble than getting some face time with a Galway hurler.'

Tom Humphries, *Laptop Dancing and the Nanny-Goat Mambo* (2003).

'It appears that I will simply have to try harder if I want to antagonise GAA officials.'

Eugene McGee, *Irish Independent* (14 May 2001).

'Galway preceptors had successful underage teams and a multiplicity of richly promising individuals to work on. And work they did: churning away with all of the diligence but none of the adroitness or intuition of some fair cailín deas crúite na mbó. So that whatever cream came to the top never quite set into a solid, wholesome block of prize-winning butter.'

Kevin Cashman, *Sunday Independent* (October 2000).

'In the history of GAA press nights, this one wins an Oscar.'

David Walsh, writing after Mayo players made a clandestine exit from a pre-arranged press night, *The Sunday Times*.

'In these times I think that too much prominence is given to the stars. Experts and sports reporters are responsible for this state of affairs. They do not give enough attention to the ordinary members of teams anymore, and I believe that this trend has a bad influence on teams and on sport in general.'

Jack Lynch, former Cork hurler and politician (1977).

'For the first half of the GAA's existence there were only a handful of full-time journalists covering GAA affairs for the national newspapers and radio. The vast majority of GAA writing was done by non-journalists who were nearly always "pure" GAA people. These GAA fans with typewriters, pencils or biros saw their main function as presenting the best possible image of their beloved GAA. Objectivity was a dirty word. Over 70 years of this "white-washing" of GAA coverage, to which there were several honourable exceptions, deluded many GAA officials into believing that they would always be able manipulate GAA coverage.'

Eugene McGee, *Irish Independent* (14 May 2001).

'The short grass man, a tower of strength in defence and a tiger in attack, stamped his mark indelibly on this game when, midway through the second moiety, he grabbed the leather, rounded the centre half-back and sent a daisy-cutter past the baffled Breffny custodian.'

Unidentified match report, quoted by Breandán Ó hEithir, *Over the Bar* (1984).

'An Fear Rua recalls the acerbic comment of the late Seán Lemass – whom history will ultimately judge as the greatest Taoiseach the State ever had – who once said *Irish Times* editorials read like they were written by "an old woman sitting in a bath, with the water cooling around her".'

Liam Cahill, responding to an *Irish Times* editorial. An Fear Rua website.

'Here in the Indo sports department, as we try to go about our daily work, the phone never stops ringing. They ring up to complain. They ring up to praise. They ring up to ask the latest score of a game being played. They ring up after Christmas every year to find out all the answers to the sports crosswords and quizzes. But mostly, after a day spent drinking and arguing in the pub, they ring up and slur the dreaded words, "Will ya settle a bet?"'

Kevin O'Shaughnessy, *Irish Independent* (1 February 2003).

'D.J.'s marital situation. Graham Geraghty's marital situation. A tabloid shrieking on the morning of a Leinster final that Dessie Farrell had been accused of drink-driving, a charge never subsequently proven. Jimmy McGuinness of Meath branded a love rat by another tabloid after he allegedly took up with another guy's girlfriend.'

Enda McEvoy, *Sunday Tribune* (25 January 2004).

'I watched the second half of the 1999 All-Ireland hurling final on the internet in a cafe in Clarke Street, Chicago. It was a crushingly lonely experience.'

Tom Humphries, *The Irish Times* (5 February 2001).

'The place was full of boys down from the mountains smelling of sheep. Inside five minutes my friend Dave Fitzgerald, his wife and my then girlfriend were busy talking to Seán. I interviewed the shepherds. I asked Seán two questions. One was, "Where did you meet your wife?" And it was at a bus stop when it was raining. Pure romance. That was my only interview, ever, ever.'

Con Houlihan, *The Back Page* (1998).

'The encouraging difference between covering GAA and the EEC is that nobody punches you in a city fish and chip shop over Monetary Compensation Amounts.'

Val Dorgan, *Irish Examiner.*

'In my career as an inter-county full-back I only once had a shot for goal and that was in the '77 semi-final. Seán Walsh moved so far outfield that once when I got the ball I found myself within scoring range. I struck for a point. But it landed on Con Houlihan. You know where Con stands, on the Canal End over at the Hogan Stand side. That's how close I came to scoring in an All-Ireland semi-final.'

Seán Doherty, interviewed by David Walsh for 'Goodbye to the Hill', *Magill* (1989).

'Your problem – in my ever so humble opinion – was that you'd dug yourself such a great big hole tipping Offaly to walk the All-Ireland that you couldn't bring yourself to the realisation of what Clare had done, to a so-called much better team!'

James A. Lundon, letter to Kevin Cashman, after the 1995 All-Ireland final, *Sunday Independent.*

'Unite, cosmhuintir of the hurling world! You have nothing to lose but your nabobs!'

Kevin Cashman, *Sunday Independent.*

'Kerry press night is all foreplay and no consummation.'

Tom Humphries, *Laptop Dancing and the Nanny-Goat Mambo* (2003).

'It is astounding that in this day and age when the GAA are constantly monitoring referees' performances that unlicensed punditry is still allowed. After all, you can't sell a hamburger outside of Croke Park without proper authority and meeting some basic hygiene regulations.'

Pól Ó Muirí, *The Irish Times* (16 August 2002).

'You saw a truly fine defender, Brian Feeney, suffering a lapse which was as shocking as hearing the Dalai Lama tell a smutty yarn or finding a split infinitive in the work of Evelyn Waugh.'

Kevin Cashman, *Sunday Independent.*

'One of the hallmarks of a Christian Brother education, apart from all the clatters on the head and clips on the ear, was learning the principal towns of every county in Ireland, their major industry (i.e. piggery), and also the official nickname of every county. The latter was essential if you ever wanted to become a GAA reporter with a local or even national newspaper, so you could write things like "after fierce pressure from the Banner men, it was looking curtains for the Breffni boys at half-time".'

Brendan Breathnach.

'The perennial Boy on the Burning Deck.'

Kevin Cashman, describing GAA PRO, Danny Lynch, *Sunday Independent.*

'They inaugurated the floodlights on a night you wouldn't let out your granny's blind cat.'

Tommy O'Callaghan, *Leinster Leader.*

'Cork's own book of current psalms.'

Micheál Ó Muircheartaigh, on the *Evening Echo*, quoted in *From Dún Síon to Croke Park* (2004).

Fourth Estate:
Broadcasters

Print journalists get a chance to think before they write (although it is hard to believe it sometimes) radio and television commentators don't. Apart from its landmark role in providing the first field broadcast of a sporting event in Europe (in 1926), the GAA has been blessed with its commentators and analysts, bards and poets, and not just the Micheál-masters – O'Hehir and Ó Muircheartaigh – and their colleagues in RTÉ, TG4, UTV, BBC and Setanta, but an army of part-time commentators in local radio stations and video productions the length and breadth of the country, divulging wisdom and other things which occasionally, but not always, relates to what is happening on the field of play.

'After the signing of the Treaty, a Provisional Government, was brought into being, and I had the honour of serving as Postmaster General. I was invited to do so by Arthur Griffith.

In due time broadcasting came into the picture, under Post Office control. Ours was, in fact, the first radio in the world to broadcast a field game, a GAA final. Equally, wherever and whenever Irish language, history and general national characteristics could have been featured, there was no hesitation in doing so.'

J.J. Walsh, First Minister for Posts in the Free State government.

'Our rugby panel of experts for televised matches always refer to players as guys. In soccer parlance we have become used to the boys. In our national games, though, we only have men. You will hear Marty Morrissey or Ger Canning talk about how the Galway men were on top but the Mayo men made a great comeback.'

Letter to *The Irish Times* (15 April 2004).

'Cork go sweeping into the Dublin goal. A cloud of dust rises. It must be a goal! Oh! Daly! Daly! Daly! Wonderful.'

P.D. Mehigan, broadcasting the 1927 All-Ireland final, quoted in Pádraig Purseil, *The GAA in Its Time* (1982).

'Holy God, it's a goal for Tipperary.'

P.D. Mehigan (attrib.).

'A Kerry man has the ball. He kicks it towards the Cavan goal. A Cavan man gets it. He kicks it out. A Kerry man gets it. He kicks it towards the Cavan goal.'

Michael Hamilton's commentary of the 1937 All-Ireland final, quoted in Con Houlihan, *Windfalls* (1997).

Micheál O'Hehir

'Bail ó Dhía oraibh go léir a cháirde agus fáilte rómhaibh go Páirc an Chrócaigh.'

Micheál O'Hehir's opening lines.

'Watching a game on the wireless was torture: a great many members of my generation would have died long ago of cardiac failure but for their salutary diet of tea and bread-and-butter and black pudding and bacon and spuds and cabbage. And Micheál O'Hehir, God love him, would have been responsible: we had to listen, torn by apprehension as opponents carried the ball towards goal: "He's gone 10 yards. He's gone 20 yards. He's gone 30 yards. He's gone 40 yards. Oh, dear God, stop him in his tracks."'

Con Houlihan.

'In the age of live championship matches every Sunday and state of the art stadium architecture, all of this may appear quaint and remote but it was Micheál O'Hehir who brought the GAA to the people and as a result into the modern world.'

Irish Times editorial (26 November 1996).

'The boy with the big hands.'

Micheál O'Hehir's name for Joe Keohane of Kerry.

'And Tom Cheasty breaks through with Kilkenny defenders falling around him like dying wasps.'

Micheál O'Hehir.

'Lovely piece of whole-hearted fielding. Mick O'Connell stretched like Nureyev for a one-handed catch.'
Micheál O'Hehir.

'And it looks like there's a bit of a schemozzle in the parallelogram.'
Mícheál O'Hehir.

'Schemozzzle is a word we all associate with Micheál. Some people are convinced that he made it up himself but that isn't so, my learned friends tell me that it is Yiddish for a "fracas".'
Con Houlihan, *Windfalls* (1997).

'The man in the cap.'
Micheál O'Hehir's name for Peter McDermott of Meath.

'Twenty-nine minutes still remaining in this game, hallelujah.'
Micheál O'Hehir, commentary of the 1977 All-Ireland semi-final between Dublin and Kerry, considered by many to be the greatest football game ever played.

Micheál Ó Muircheartaigh

'It was a help that the adjudicators could not see the pitch.'
Micheál Ó Muircheartaigh, on his trial broadcast for Radio Éireann in 1949, *From Dún Síon to Croke Park* (2004).

'No known roof is as beautiful as the skies above.'
Micheál Ó Muircheartaigh, *From Dún Síon to Croke Park* (2004).

'He can take the ball from one end of the field to the other with just the player's occupations.'

Jack O'Shea, on Micheál Ó Muircheartaigh.

'You get the impression that Micheál Ó Muircheartaigh is on personal terms with their brothers and sisters, parents and grandparents. He was able to tell us that Kilkenny midfield debutant Conor Phelan and his twin brother John went to school in Roscrea. At one stage, he named out all of Damien Fitzhenry's fourteen brothers and sisters. He also reminisced about a Duffrey Rovers football team populated by numerous Fitzhenrys playing at Croke Park on a day in which Seamus Fitzhenry almost scored the goal of the year.'

Liam Cahill.

'The Dodger has it. The Dodger is moving in. A shot from the Dodger and it's gone over the bar – another point for Kilkenny. In case you came in from Mars today, the Dodger is D.J. Carey of Gowran and Kilkenny.'

Micheál Ó Muircheartaigh.

'Anthony Lynch the Cork corner-back will be the last person to let you down... his people are undertakers.'

Micheál Ó Muircheartaigh.

'He grabs the sliotar, he's on the 50, he's on the 40, he's on the 30, he's on the ground.'

Micheál Ó Muircheartaigh.

'Teddy looks at the ball, the ball looks at Teddy.'

Micheál Ó Muircheartaigh, on Teddy McCarthy of Cork.

'Pat Fox out to the 40 and grabs the sliotar, I bought a dog from his father last week. Fox turns and sprints for goal, the dog ran a great race last Tuesday in Limerick. Fox to the 21, fires a shot, it goes to the left and wide... and the dog lost as well.'

Micheál Ó Muircheartaigh.

'There's a streaker on the pitch – he must be a Kilkenny man because he's quite happy with the situation right now. If the streaker doesn't mind, the ball will be going over in his direction right now. He sees the danger – now he's moving out the field towards open territory. The stewards are moving in on him now. He's now gone past the centre of the field. Níl fhios agam cad as a tháinig sé. He's dodging his way now trying to get away from the maors. He's made a good run. He's on the 50-yard line on the other side of the field. He's brought to the ground. Tá an streaker ag imeacht den bpáirc.'

Micheál Ó Muircheartaigh, during 2003 Leinster final.

'1–5 to 0–8 well from Lapland to the Antarctic, that's level scores in any man's language.'

Micheál Ó Muircheartaigh.

'In the first half they played with the wind. In the second half they played with the ball.'

Micheál Ó Muircheartaigh.

'And Brian Dooher is down injured. And while he is, I'll tell ye a little story. I was in Times Square in New York last week, and I was missing the Championship back home. So I approached a news stand and I said, "I suppose ye wouldn't have *The Kerryman* would ye?" To which, the Egyptian behind the counter turned to me and he said, "Do you want the North Kerry edition or the South Kerry edition?" He had both... so I bought both. And Dooher is back on his feet.'

Micheál Ó Muircheartaigh.

'Colin Corkery on the 45 lets go with the right boot. It's over the bar. This man shouldn't be playing football. He's made an almost Lazarus-like recovery from a heart condition. Lazarus was a great man but he couldn't kick points like Colin Corkery.'

Micheál Ó Muircheartaigh.

'Stephen Byrne with the puck out for Offaly, Stephen, one of twelve, all but one are here today, the one that's missing is Mary, she's at home minding the house, and the ball is dropping i lár na bpáirce.'

Micheál Ó Muircheartaigh.

'Danny "The Yank" Culloty. He came down from the mountains and hasn't he done well.'

Micheál Ó Muircheartaigh.

'If he hits the ball like he did in the first half, this will end up in Clonliffe College. Yes, it's gone over Hill 16 and out over the railway. That sliotar will play no more hurling today.'

Micheál Ó Muircheartaigh, on Paul Codd.

'I saw a few Sligo people at Mass in Gardiner Street this morning and the omens seem to be good for them, the priest was wearing the same colours as the Sligo jersey. Forty yards out on the Hogan Stand side of the field Dublin's

Ciaran Whelan goes on a rampage, it's a goal! So much for religion.'

Micheál Ó Muircheartaigh.

'He kicks the ball lán san aer, could've been a goal, could've been a point, it went wide.'

Micheál Ó Muircheartaigh.

'Seán Óg Ó hAilpín, his father's from Fermanagh, his mother's from Fiji – neither a hurling stronghold.'

Micheál Ó Muircheartaigh.

'Teddy McCarthy to John McCarthy, no relation. John McCarthy back to Teddy McCarthy, still no relation.'

Micheál Ó Muircheartaigh.

Eddie Moroney

'That referee must have no wipers on his glasses!'

Eddie Moroney, in his commentary on the 1992 Tipperary Under-21 county football final, Aherlow vs Éire Óg Nenagh.

'It's definitely probably one of the greatest days in Aherlow in GAA circumstances.'

'He gave him a belt after the ball. He's all right. He's only winded.'

'It's in the back of the net, but there's a free out to be taken by, I dunno.'

'The referee is looking around and acting the mickey!'

'Brian Connolly... Kenneally... Connolly... Will ya kick the ball!'

'He's giving a penalty! The bollocks has given a penalty.'

'Jaysus, I think I am going to get sick after that beer yesterday, I'm not well.'

'Me false teeth are coming out!'

'He got a boot in the head, it's on the camera you can't miss it.'

'It comes back to what the hell is his name again.'

'And the game is over. What a victory. Oh mother of God there'll be a big night in the Glen.'

More lines from Eddie Moroney's commentary on 1992 Tipperary Under-21 county football final.

And the Rest

'There won't be a cow milked in Clare tonight.'

Marty Morrissey, after Clare's 1992 Munster football championship win.

'There won't be a cow milked in Finglas tonight.'

Keith Bar of Erin's Isle, after the club qualified for the 1998 All-Ireland club football final.

'The cigarettes are being lit here in the commentary box. The lads are getting anxious. It's a line ball down there to Clare and who is to take it?... Will ye put 'em out lads! Ye'll choke me.'

Matthew McMahon of Clare FM, during the 1995 All-Ireland hurling final.

'It's all over. Clare are – Jeeeesus.'
Matthew McMahon of Clare FM, at the end of the 1995
Munster final.

'The biggest criticism I get is for not giving the score often
enough. Funnily enough, I had someone complain about that
after the Munster club hurling game between Kilmaley and
Mount Sion, which the Waterford champions won well. But
then he said: "I knew by the sound of you that it wasn't
good."'
Matthew McMahon of Clare FM.

'Ollie Murphy is after throwing so many dummies, you
wouldn't see the likes in a creche.'
Kevin Mallon, of LM/FM local radio.

'Pick the bones out of that Mrs McGuinness.'
Barry Henriques, of KCLR 96FM.

'The most versatile sportsman of them all AN Other is a late
withdrawal from the Limerick team.'
Mal Keaveney, of Limerick's Live 95FM.

'I don't want to be biased but what was the referee at there?'
Seán Walsh, of Galway Bay FM.

'The fat lady can start singing.'
Paudie Palmer, of Cork 103FM County Sound.

'The referee offers a shrill blast of the whistle.'
John Cashman, of Cork 103FM County Sound.

'The modh díreach.'

Mike Finnerty, of Mid-West Radio.

'The sun is blowing diagonally across the field.'

Mick Dunne, on RTÉ Radio.

'Giving the television commentary of last Sunday's minor hurling championship game between Galway and Tipperary in English rather than Irish was a decision taken by RTÉ without agreement with the Association. The GAA has formally communicated with RTÉ informing them that it wishes to continue its traditional policy of applying Irish commentaries in its live television transmission of the All-Ireland minor hurling and football championships.'

GAA statement, after the commentary of the 2001 minor hurling championship semi-final was broadcast in English, reported in the *Irish Independent*.

Fourth Estate:

Analysts

Like old-time vaudeville, television studios thrive on the collaboration between a straight guy and a comedian. For much of the history of the GAA, television was distant from the rural heartlands where the games were strongest, and straight-talking analysts were difficult to come by. Thankfully, all has changed. With as much attention being paid to analysis as to match action, the words of those ex-players and managers selected for studio performance have taken on added importance. Some of them are even wise.

'Joe Brolly in full flight, on the field or off it.'
Weblog, 101 reasons why the GAA is better than soccer.

'I don't expect it to be open, I don't expect it to be attractive. As we know Ulster teams tend to have a negative influence on Gaelic football in general.'
Colm O'Rourke.

Micheal Lyster: 'Are Donegal's streamlined jerseys so opponents couldn't grab a hold of them?'

Joe Brolly: 'No, they're strictly for the girls, non-stick jerseys.'

Joe Brolly: 'Armagh were like a German Panzer division, they just rolled over Donegal.'

Colm O'Rourke: 'Armagh won't thank you, you shouldn't have mentioned Panzer divisions – they got wiped out.'

Joe Brolly: 'But only when they ran out of oil, and there's a plentiful supply of that in South Armagh.'

Colm O'Rourke: 'Maybe they're trying to keep Laois waiting in the sun, a bit like Kerry last year.'

Joe Brolly: 'Or maybe they're sitting in there with some custard creams.'

Joe Brolly: 'You'd have thought there was a fatwah out on me.'

Colm O'Rourke: 'There is.'

'The worst thing about the game was there wasn't even a chance of a row.'

Colm O'Rourke.

'Hell hath no fury like an Ulster football supporter.'

Joe Brolly.

'If it's a good game it'll be the first and I'll believe it when I see it – the Ulster championship has been pitiful... [Seventy minutes later] I'm glad to be able to say something nice about an Ulster final: it was a very entertaining game.'

Colm O'Rourke.

'Brolly accuses Tom Kelly of getting Alan Barry sent off in the Leinster final. I would like to make it clear that Tom Kelly was not responsible for Alan Barry's dismissal.'

Declan Byrne, secretary of Laois club St Joseph's.

'You may talk about this match until the cows come home but at the end of the day there was only a puck of a ball between the teams.'

Michael Lyster, RTÉ presenter on 1986 All-Ireland hurling final.

'Tyrone have a lot of bad players. Brian Dooher is a bad player. I have a very expensive hat and I will eat it on this show if Tyrone win an All-Ireland and Brian Dooher is on the team.'

Colm O'Rourke (2003).

'With the sort of stomach O'Rourke has he could probably digest it.'

Joe Brolly.

'The agony, the ecstasy and the difficulty of eating a straw hat.'

Michael Lyster, after Tyrone won the All-Ireland in 2003, with Dooher on the team.

'They were saying nice things to me – I preferred it when they hated me.'

Joe Brolly.

'The real problem with the foot and mouth epidemic, Pat, is that you didn't get it.'

Ted Walsh, to Pat Spillane.

'They have a forward line that couldn't punch holes in a paper bag.'

Pat Spillane, on the 1997 Cavan football team.

'Joe Brolly always talked a great game. The problem was that he didn't always play a great one.'

Colm O'Rourke.

'Repent or I shall send thee down a darkened alley with the free-scoring Derry forwards, coached by none other than moi.'

Joe Brolly.

'Identify the Derry captain. Anthony Hopkins, Anthony Clare or Anthony Tohill.'

Sunday Game competition on RTÉ.

'If I had Ronan Quinn marking me, I think that I'd beat him for pace... he's like a fish out of water at corner-back. He's slow and ponderous at full-back, he's even slower and more ponderous at corner-back.'

Pat Spillane.

'I swear to God, my mother would be faster than most of those three fellas and she has a bit of arthritis in the knee.'

Pat Spillane, describing the Armagh full-back line at half-time during the 2002 All-Ireland final. Armagh went on win.

'Are you watching, Pat Spillane?'
Banner at 2002 All-Ireland final.

'A lot of neutrals would say these games are a turn-off, but it's a bit like going to a chic restaurant nowadays and seeing sort of fried goat's intestines on the menu and saying "yuck", and it turns out that it's the best dish they have.'
Pat Spillane.

'I've puked after beer, but that doesn't say I've lost my liking for beer.'
Pat Spillane.

'We won't be getting many highlights out of this game, unless O'Rourke and myself do a strip in the next few seconds.'
Pat Spillane.

'Spillane was an outstanding footballer, but like Charlie Haughey, he is in real danger of being remembered for all the wrong reasons. It's too late for C.J. and time is running out for Pat.'
Emmett Moloney, *The Kerryman* (2002).

'If Karl O'Dwyer was in Kerry he wouldn't be making the Kerry senior championship side, if Brian Murphy was in Cork, he wouldn't be making the Cork junior football side.'
Pat Spillane.

'The Cork junior footballers are safe!'
Pat Spillane in 2002, before Kildare beat Dublin in the Leinster final.

'What is this about Kildare forwards, the sheep down in Connemara know this about them, passing tourists in Kildare can shout out the window at people, you can't score. Why is this?'
Pat Spillane.

'How can you talk logic and analyse a game when you're talking about Kildare.'
Tony Davis.

'The first half was even, the second half was even worse.'
Pat Spillane, quoting Mick 'Rattler' Byrne of Tipperary.

'You might be better off watching *Buffy the Vampire Slayer* on the other channel.'
Pat Spillane.

Take one: 'I'd say between every one of the counties in Munster there's a huge rivalry and when you do beat someone you enjoy it – in the same way that when you lose it, it... Are you still rolling? I was going to say it "hurts" but we can't say that, full-backs don't say "hurt".'

Take two: 'And when you lose, it [silence] isn't very pleasant.'
Brian Lohan, *Breaking Ball*.

'Dublin have been knocked down on the floor twice in two minutes, we'll see what they are made of now.'
Tony Davis.

'Bhí sé down to the wire.'
Fiona Corcoran on TG4 after a women's All-Ireland semi-final.

'The first goal, from Dermot Earley, was actually worth more than its three points. Dublin never recovered.'
Colm O'Rourke.

'It was like raining stones. You wouldn't know what to make of it.'
Cyril Farrell, commenting on the ball ricocheting 5 times off Brendan Cummins.

'It's a poison through the game, we just can't have it... are we going to end up spitting over each other?'
Joe Brolly, on gamesmanship in the Ulster final.

'Henry Shefflin. You don't want to mark him if you have only one leg.'
Ger Loughnane.

'They lost nothing today – except pride and, of course, the Connacht title.'
Marty Morrissey.

'I'd say there's not one person in the stadium who went to the toilet today.'
Larry O'Gorman.

'We've [Kerry] had 32 great Sundays in Croke Park. It's not in any manual... appetite, hunger, will to win. We'll be slagged off for what we said at half-time... inept Armagh... whatever Joe [Kernan] said at half-time should be bottled.'
Pat Spillane.

'Benny Coulter has a left foot in the right place.'
Colm O'Rourke.

'He drove it hard but it seemed to elevate at the wrong moment.'
Marty Morrissey, bemoaning a Tyrone goal attempt that seemed to hit some midair turbulence.

'I bumped in to some Derry supporters in the toilets in Clones and heard them discussing where it had all gone wrong. And that was while the game was still on.'
Michael Lyster.

'Marty Morrissey becomes a figurehead to the nation at times of true crisis in the darker provinces of the GAA. And there is the sense that, with Marty at the helm, the final resolution will be a happy one. This is because Moz, far from wanting to sensationalise crisis stories, genuinely wants a peaceful outcome.'
Keith Duggan, on the 1998 incident when it was mistakenly reported that Colin Lynch's grandmother had died during a suspension appeal, *The Irish Times* (3 April 2002).

'Last Monday, Colin's grandmother, whose pride and joy Colin was, sadly had a stroke and unfortunately just a few hours ago, she was taken off a life-support machine. So you will understand that Colin cannot be here tonight. Whatever happens here tonight pales into insignificance compared to what has happened to his family over the last few weeks.'
Ger Loughnane.

'Where's Morrissey?'

Ger Loughnane, striding through a hotel after a broadcast by RTÉ's Marty Morrissey suggested that Colin Lynch's grandmother had died.

'Now I wasn't entirely blameless either, because when I made the statement going in, I should have said she was gone off all her medication instead of saying she was gone off her machine.'

Ger Loughnane.

'"You're the radio man?" "That's me." "Well, if it is you, you've never said a good word about Westmeath in your life."'

Sean Óg Ó Ceallachain.

'Armagh could have posted a letter to Laois during the week saying exactly what they were going to do and they would still do just that.'

Colm O'Rourke.

'We are going to have a really hard – hard now – game and that is what we want.'

Ger Loughnane.

'Thurles to me is the home of hurling. I have a sneaky feeling Kilkenny will get through. Most neutrals will feel that Clare lost their chance.'

Ger Loughnane.

'It's like plucking apples off a neighbour's [silence] apple tree.'

Ger Canning, on J.J. Delaney.

'The ruin has rained the game.'
Jimmy Smyth, BBC Northern Ireland.

'Aaaah!'
Eamonn Cregan, in the Thurles commentary box as Damien Quigley blazed his kick high and wide of Davy Fitz's upright in the 1995 Munster final.

GAA Phrasebook

The cries from the battlefield often require interpretation. Below are some of the key phrases used during the course of a match, taken from a weblog.

a hang sangwidge – consumed with tay on the sides of roads after matches in Croker or Thurles.

a right [*insert expletive*] – the referee was a bit biased towards the other team.

báite – I put a fair bit of effort into it, e.g. 'I gave it báite.'

blast – a great amount of anything.

bomber – a very popular nickname for a GAA player.

brawl – a collection of bodies in disagreement with each other.

bullin – angry, e.g. 'The centre half-back was bullin after I lamped him.'

bull thick – very angry.

bushted – broken, e.g. 'Jayz me arm is bushted.'

citeog – left-handed/footed, e.g. 'He hit it with his citeog.'

dinger – usually a fast wing-forward who can leave his opponent for dust.

flakin – usually goes on for a whole game, e.g. 'Mike Murphy gave Tony Delaney an awful flakin below in training on Sunday.'

hames – a right mess, e.g. 'He made a hames of that clearance.'

hape/heap – a big quantity.

horse – untidy or rough player, there's one in every club (the legendary Horse Delaney).

horsed – bout of rough play or intimidatory tactics, e.g. 'We horsed them out of it.'

in the paw – to catch the ball.

joshel – a shoulder push.

lamp – a good thump.

leh-it-in-ta-would-ya – Full-forwards appeal to a midfielder for a more timely delivery of the pass.

Lord lantern Jaysus – 'The next time you do that, I'll kill ya.'

mighty – very good.

mullocker – untidy or awkward players.

namajaysus – 'What was that for, ref?'

rake – also a great amount of anything, usually pints of Guinness.

row – fight involving four or more players swinging hurleys like lunatics.

massive row – row involving both team, substitutes and supporters jumping fences.

running row – a massive row that continues out in the parking area and/or dressing-room areas.

schkelp – a good thump.

schemozzle – a group of players schkelping one another but not exactly hitting anyone at the same time.

stomached – surprised, e.g. 'When he came up behind me I was awful stomached.'

the comm-it-eeee – local GAA chancers in general.

timber – intimidation of a hurling opponent.

warp – hit something hard.

welt – swing at.

Kerry Fans
and Other Animals

'Being a Kerry manager is probably the hardest job in the world because Kerry people, I'd say, are the roughest type of f***ing animals you could ever deal with. And you can print that.'

Páidí Ó Sé, *Sunday Independent* (January 2003).

'In west Kerry, the term "animal" is not as offensive as it is perhaps to the more Anglicised, uppish people in towns such as Killarney. Animal as it was understood in Irish, was a being close to the human. Humans were animals with souls.'

Canon Pádraig Ó Fiannachta of Ventry.

'Canon Pádraig Ó Fiannachta cannot have consulted Éamonn Ó hÓgáin's *Díolaim Focal (A) Ó Chorca Dhuibhne* in which a long entry on the word "ainmhí" distinguishes three subsidiary meanings referring to people: (a) boor; (b) noisy, obstreperous, person; and (c) pitiless person. Perhaps it is just as well that the county board did not consider the possibility of a Gaelic connection or they might have been less ready to settle with Páidí. Perhaps the real cause of the problem is not Irish influence on the meaning of the word "animal" but that most global of English words: the *f*-word. I conclude with relief that the Irish language must be acquitted of all blame.'

Diarmuid Ó Se, Department of Modern Irish, in a letter to *The Irish Times* (25 January 2003).

'What I meant in the article about the Kerry supporters is that they are very hard to please, always demanding the highest standards, because they are a very proud race of people… From time to time, I unfortunately go about describing things the wrong way, and I regret and apologise to the people of Kerry if I have hurt, disturbed or upset them in any way.'

Páidí Ó Sé (January 2003).

'The man had a few pints in him and he was caught by a crafty Dublin journalist. His language was inappropriate and he was quoted verbatim. He is a rough man and he speaks roughly especially after a couple of pints. And the comment itself about the Kerry supporters and the animal part of it, he did not mean that at all, I know that for a fact. It was strong language but what Páidí meant was that they are critical and demanding, which he says in his apology.'

Liam Higgins, talking on Radio Kerry (January 2003).

'I could not believe what I saw in *The Kerryman* a few days later with more expletives and then this *Sunday Independent* interview with a couple of more *f*s. I think it is not right for the manager or trainer of the Kerry team to be saying those things. I think you are representing Kerry and if you take a job like that there are three groups of people you have to be loyal to. They are, number one, the selectors that are in there with you, the players, whom you have to look after, and lastly the supporters. You need to have those three groups together and on your side.'

Ger Power, talking on Radio Kerry (January 2003).

'We admit to having checked the football record books and were amazed to see how Kerry won All-Irelands during the Year of the Ox, the Year of the Tiger, the Year of the Monkey... By Christ! Páidí was right all along. They are f***ing animals down there.'

Sheepstealers.com, the Roscommon fans' website.

Kingdom Came:
The Great Team of 1975–1987

Time has delivered its verdict that Kerry's second four in a row team, 1978–1981, was the greatest of all time. It might have been nine All-Irelands in succession, 1978 to 1986 – but they were rattled by two last-minute goals in the championships of 1982 and 1983, two years when Kerry were over-whelming favourites to win. And the nucleus of that team came back to win another three in a row.

'Meath bet the lard out of us in the quarter-finals of the national league [in 1975], and Micko took over after that.'
Mikey Sheehy.

'The team's inexperience frightened me. To compensate, I wanted to have them wound up to a pitch where they would go through fire and water to win a 50–50 ball. We needed that kind of spirit to stand any chance against Dublin.'
Mick O'Dwyer, Kerry manager in the 1970s and 1980s.

'Ger McKenna gave me a free rein with the team. "Do it your way," he said. I told him we had great potential, perhaps we would win the All-Ireland in three years. It came straight-away. There'll never be another 1975.'

Mick O'Dwyer, Kerry manager in the 1970s and 1980s.

'Paddy put on a show of righteous indignation that would get him a card from Equity, throwing up his hands to heaven as the referee kept pointing to the goal. And while all of this was going on, Mike Sheehy came running up to take the kick – and suddenly Paddy dashes back like a woman who smells a cake burning. The ball won the race and it curled inside the near post as Paddy crashed into the outside of the net and lay against it like a fireman who had returned to find his station ablaze. Some time Noel Pearson may make a musical of this final – and as the green flag goes up for that crazy goal he will have a banshee's voice crooning, "And that was the end of poor Molly Malone." So it was. A few min-utes later came the tea break. Kerry went in to a frenzy of green and gold and a tumult of acclaim. The champions looked like men who had worked hard and seen their sav-ings plundered by bandits. The great rain robbers were out onto the field for Act Two.'

Con Houlihan, describing the 1978 All-Ireland final Mikey Sheehy–Paddy Cullen goal in a classic piece from the *Evening Press*.

'I saw the way the way Dublin played in '74 and I decided that the only way to go was to get a gang of young players who would be exceptionally fit and supple and the whole lot. It was a gamble, but I wanted to build a new team and coach them and train them the way I wanted to do it. They were all young guys and they were mad to be part of it. They were willing to go through any barriers.'

Mick O'Dwyer, with his panel picked, he trained them for 27 nights, non-stop, every night.

'Mick O'Dwyer was sitting in the dug-out like a woman who has a big family scattered around Britain and America and gets money in every post.'

Con Houlihan, *Evening Press*.

'They were all really lucky goals. Seán Doherty was marking me and at one point I just moved away from him to get a bit of a break from his attention. The next thing the ball landed in my hands and I was clear.'

Eoin Liston (1978).

'We were 0–6 to 0–1 behind and the doubt was just starting to creep in… In a football sense they had beaten us around the field in the first half and to be honest we were in real trouble. But before the break John Egan got a goal to get us back in the game and then of course Mike Sheehy did his famous lob over Paddy Cullen. At the time I wasn't even sure if it was allowed, I went into the dressing room at half-time thinking we were a point down.'

Eoin Liston (1978).

'We really had a team. Dublin hit us with everything, and so did Offaly and Roscommon and all of them. We met them all in our time and it made no difference one way or the other. I mean we had so much power and skill that we never had to bother about the other teams. The one thing we had, we were able to go and win the ball. Ball, number one. It wasn't about stopping other teams from playing. We played our own game and let the other team do what they like.'

Mick O'Dwyer, Kerry manager in the 1970s and 1980s.

'You'll see great individual players, of course you will, but you won't see a team of that quality again – I don't believe you will anyway.'

Mick O'Dwyer, Kerry manager in the 1970s and 1980s.

'Five in a row, five in a row/It's hard to believe we've won five in a row.'

Ballad to commemorate Kerry victory in the 1982 All-Ireland, recorded in advance by folk group Galleon. Kerry lost.

'Five in a row, five in a row, Christ we were close to five in a row.'

Eoin Liston of Kerry's two-line ballad (1982).

'Don't for one minute think that we were going to get bored with it. Winning All-Irelands! I was born in a place called Sneem. Any fella who had any ambition, it was to play for Kerry. There was no soccer, no hurling, no nothing. And to play for Kerry was the dream. I got on a successful Kerry team that won All-Irelands. Why should a fella get off it? The power and the glory!'

John Egan.

'We trained in Killarney and people came from all over the country to look at us and watch us training. There used to be hundreds in there. People on their holidays in Kerry, they used to come down in the evenings and watch us. And everywhere we went there was thousands came to our games. Even during the Troubles in the North, we went up there to raise money for a tour, we got massive gates and massive crowds. They were marvellous players but they were so accessible as people.'

Mick O'Dwyer, Kerry manager in the 1970s and 1980s.

'Certainly it would be harder to win now but that team would win All-Irelands in any period, I've no doubt in my mind about that. Those guys had unbelievable skill. Jaysus I mean, if you think of Ger Power, Ogie Moran and Spillane, and then with Sheehy, Liston and Egan inside. God Almighty. If you had them in on a team today, they'd still destroy defenders. And I'll tell you, bringing fifteen men behind the ball wouldn't matter against them fellas because they'd still be well capable of winning it [the ball]. Winning it and turning and scoring as well. I mean they were deadly accurate. They could kick points from anywhere. And how many teams today can do that? Not too many.'

Mick O'Dwyer, Kerry manager in the 1970s and 1980s.

'An entrepreneur from London came over to Dublin a week before the All-Ireland and he was selling five in a row T-shirts. He was a good Kerry man. He got RIP written across the T-shirts and he sold the T-shirts in Offaly.'

Páidí Ó Sé, quoted in Colm Keane, *A Cut Above the Rest* (1999).

'Kerry played possession football to an extraordinary degree and almost lost. Mick O'Dwyer must have felt like a hen that hatched out a clutch of eggs and found herself mothering ducklings.'

Con Houlihan, on the 1986 All-Ireland.

'And it's up the gallant Kingdom/And up the great O'Dwyer /The Kingdom's greatest trainer/Whose skills we all admire/ We'll toast our Kerry heroes/Who brought our county fame /And thank them for their victory/In this very sporting game.'

Kerry supporters' ballad (1981).

'Never was so much achieved on the pitch for so many years by so few.'

Cork Examiner editorial on the 1975–1987 Kerry team.

'At the time I didn't think any of them would be legends. I mean the only thing that I had on my mind at that stage was to try and beat Cork in a Munster final. And they managed to beat them in Killarney and that was the stepping stone to greatness after.'

Mick O'Dwyer, Kerry manager in the 1970s and 1980s.

'The circus is over, it's time for a new act.'

Eoin Liston, Kerry full-forward, speaking after Kerry's defeat in 1987.

Ladies Who Play
(and a man)

The silent majority of our population had a long struggle for recognition before Gaelic football and camogie became the two best supported women's field games in Europe, with television viewerships regularly exceeding men's rugby internationals. With over a hundred years of camogie and 30 years of football, they have their share of witticisms, cross words and kind words.

'Bright shone the sunlight on Peggy and Doreen/Wild swing the ash sticks. Be careful a stóirín/Josie is getting right into their stride now/Kathleen is hurling with all her Cork pride now/A shout from the sideline: mark your man Kathleen Cody Kathleen pucks it, I tell you that puck was dotie./The game is exciting, it is indeed really/Maureen Cashman is tackling bold Ide O'Kiely.'

Patrick Kavanagh, 'Camogie Match'.

'Chicks with sticks.'
Promotional slogan for camogie (2002).

'I believe "chick" is a derogatory word when used for women because its specific definition is something other than intelligent, mature, full human beings.'
Letter to *The Irish Times* (16 May 2003).

'What would she have him use? Humans of the Female Gender with Sticks has a nice ring to it.'
Letter to *The Irish Times* (17 May 2003).

'Under-18 and under-21 grades in camogie in Dublin would halve the city's drink problem in a stroke of the pen.'
Tom Humphries, *The Irish Times* (26 May 2003).

'The GAA may not appreciate its women as much as it should but at least we all know who Angela Downey is. The most famous woman in English soccer is Posh Spice.'
Weblog, 101 reasons why the GAA is better than soccer.

'First of all, I'd like to thank all the players. Without them we wouldn't be here.'
Liz O'Dwyer, Tipperary captain.

'I can recall some of the early matches when each player wielded her camog at her own sweet will without any reference to her colleagues, just to show how far she could put a ball. The ball could fall anywhere, usually out among the spectators who took it all in good humour while the proud wielder of the camog felt she had gone one better than her brothers on the hurling field.'

Agnes O'Farrelly, speaking about early camogie quoted in Pádraig Purseil, *The GAA in Its Time* (1982).

'Camóguidheacht.'

Tadhg Ó Donnchadha, inventing a new game from the word camóg.

'And then there was the time of the hobble skirts, when the girls went down like nine pins when they tried to run.'

Agnes O'Farrelly, speaking about early camogie.

'You wonder what did you do before the season began. It's hard to remember.'

Liz O'Dwyer, Tipperary captain.

'Besides their performances on the pitch, what kind of qualities do these girls have that makes you want to spend so much of your time with them?'

Jim Carney, speaking to Tipperary's male coach.

'The best and most passionate hurling of all of 1986 was served up by Glen Rovers and St Paul's in the club camogie final. Scores born of rare and profound artistry abounded.'

Kevin Cashman, on the 1986 All-Ireland camogie club final in which Glen Rovers beat St Paul's 4–11 to 5–7, *Sunday Independent.*

'It's disappointing that that's what it takes for women's sport to get attention. It's never about your ability or anything like

that. A lot of the players didn't like it. We just thought, my God, we're not like that – we can dress up, we can be glamorous, but let's not make a big point of it. When we saw the photos we just said, for feck's sake, what are they making us out to be?'
Eimear McDonnell (23 January 2004).

'Bridesmaids no more! That was the catch cry of Laois' lady footballers when they finally obliterated the ghosts of their seven heartbreaking previous losses to win their first senior title.'
Irish Independent (2002).

'For most of September it had appeared that Croke Park would see out the season with nothing but lob-sided football matches. Then the senior women of Laois and Mayo came along for their say, and ended up producing one of the most intensely exciting games that the GAA's headquarters has ever witnessed.'
Ian O'Riordan, *The Irish Times* (2002).

'There's a lot of pious old rubbish talked about women in sport but the Ashbourne Cup is one of those traditions that needs no patronage or piety.'
Tom Humphries, *The Irish Times* (9 February 2004).

'Everywhere I go now I see hordes of kids carrying hurleys. Girls as often as boys. From Cabra to Donnycarney to Marino to Ballyboden to Kilmacud, girls are doing unbelievable things, they are moulding themselves into teams, expressing themselves, challenging themselves, pushing themselves. I see fathers out pucking sliotars around with their daughters until the girls give permission to head for home. I see girls fighting over whose sideline cut it is, arguing with refs, soloing 40 yards, executing perfect blocks. Just enjoying the best sport in the world.'

Tom Humphries, *The Irish Times* (12 May 2003).

'I can't remember playing with anything else when I was young, only a hurley and ball, never a doll.'

Marian McCarthy of Cork, quoted in Brendan Fullam, *Hurling Giants* (1994).

'It requires the willing dismantlement of the Berlin Wall which camogie and hurling cliques like to put up around themselves. It means looking out your clubhouse window some days and seeing the minor football team training in a corner and the under-13 camogie team playing on the main pitch.'

Tom Humphries, *The Irish Times* (22 September 2003).

'I reckon that a lady's or a girl's body is too precious to be abused, bumped and humped playing football. Their bodies are not made for humps and bumps. They have their own natural humps and bumps.'

Malachy Byrne, opposing a □,065 grant from Roscommon VEC for promotion of football, quoted in John Scally, Sporting Foot and Mouth (2002).

'When my friends were besotted with Jason Donovan, my heroes were Colm O'Rourke and Barney Rock.'

Sue Ramsbottom, Laois ladies captain.

'Ah! I gnash my hair and tear out my teeth by the handful that I have just missed one of the greatest sporting events of recent times – and it so close to my home! I speak of course of the camogie match between Kiltegan and Annacurra in Pearse Park in Arklow the weekend before last, in which all thirty players became involved in a savage brawl: fists, boots and camáns. When the encounter began to resemble the Third Battle of Ypres (though without any of the mercy which occasionally illuminated that melancholy encounter) the referee, Martina Kennedy, sent all thirty players to the dressing rooms – no doubt with much booing from the spectators, who were only just getting warmed up.'

Kevin Myers, *The Irish Times* (16 July 2004).

'Pass me the ball, mammy.'

Siobhan McAtmney to her Aunt Maura in the Ulster Club camogie final in 1978, quoted in Brendan Fullam, *Legends of the Ash* (1997).

'I have long wondered why so many mná are active members of GAA clubs, and are not putting that energy to the development of their own codes which seemingly lack volunteers, and also why so many men – not members of any GAA club – can find the time to administer in ladies' football. If each attended to their own sports, would it not be to the advantage of both codes?'

Paul Donaghy, *Carlow Nationalist.*

'I forgot to thank our sponsors, the *Horse and Jockey*. They're great like.'

Liz O'Dwyer, Tipperary captain.

'The tragedy of camogie is that it has suffered for too long from its image of being something for big girls with fat ankles to do between Macra dances. It has no face, no stars, no real impact on those who don't play it or know it.'

Tom Humphries, *The Irish Times* (12 May 2003).

'What I am looking forward to is witnessing the continued adventures of the St Vincent's under-11 B camogie team. No other team gives as much entertainment for your sporting dollar, no other side gives as much commitment, no other team has my two kids on it. They are restoring the family name, wiping away the legacy of the father whose con-tributions to the junior B grade were instrumental in the setting up of a junior C grade, which was mainly made up of victims of landmines and yours truly.'

Tom Humphries, *The Irish Times* (7 January 2002).

'Kildare had a player that was a bit suspicious. I thought the legs weren't right, and the way she pulled on the ball on a couple of occasions. I knew she was wearing a wig. She dis-appeared very quickly after the match, a soldier form the Curragh I believe.'

Kathleen Mills, 15-time All-Ireland medallist, quoted in Brendan Fullam, *Hurling Giants* (1994).

Ladies Who Wait

The men's games have benefited from the support of a small army of women, and not just the wives and mothers, who influenced the great hurlers and footballers in their own ways.

'My mother was the kind of woman who wouldn't let you sit in a draught but when you were playing hurling you could play in a downpour and everything was all right.'
Jimmy Smyth of Clare, quoted in Colm Keane, *Hurling's Top Twenty* (2002).

'She cheers our team, her eyes aflame/And after Sunday's final game/I'll meet her in a glen I'll name/And ask her to the altar.'
P.D. Mehigan, 'The Lass that Loves a Hurler'.

'Anytime I was sent off I used to think of my mother: "God almighty, what's she going to be thinking of now."'
Liam Dunne.

'Their mother, Emeli, would stand underneath them goal-tending, refereeing, threatening the sanction of No Dinner for anyone who flaked too hard or tried too little.'

Tom Humphries, writing on the Ó hAilpíns, *The Irish Times* (13 September 2003).

'Mum would go goal. She's no Brendan Cummins but she'd get something to it. Too many goals and it's no dinner. So we'd go for points. There's no flaking like what we did to each other out there.'

Seán Óg Ó hAilpín.

'My mother, being a great GAA enthusiast, registered me on the 1st of January even though I was born on the 29th of December. The 1st of January gave me an extra year as a minor. That's what gave me the edge.'

Jimmy Smyth of Clare, quoted in Colm Keane, *Hurling's Top Twenty* (2002).

'It's a huge disappointment when the team loses. It affects the whole family. There is literally a depression. People not involved in the sport wouldn't understand.'

Sinead Dooley, wife of Offaly's Johnny Dooley.

'Do you know, missus, your son is the best hurler in Ireland.'

Christy Ring to Jimmy Smyth's mother, quoted in Colm Keane, *Hurling's Top Twenty* (2002).

'My mother would never go to the games. She would listen to them on the radio. She would never praise if I scored but would always remind me of the ones I missed. After the 1956

final against Wexford she said, "Pity you didn't win. Uncle Tommy had three All-Ireland medals the same as yourself."'
Paddy Barry of Cork, quoted in Brendan Fullam, *Hurling Giants* (1994).

'The Ladies Committee: Great for sandwiches and tea after the big games always bring finer touch to club noting that ashtrays should never be left full in the bar.'
Weblog.

'My mother was up in the stand saying the rosary, although it didn't do us any good.'
Billy Rackard, commenting on the 1951 All-Ireland final, quoted in Colm Keane, *Hurling's Top Twenty* (2002).

'My mother used to clean off the clay from around the clogs of my boots into the geranium pots. She used to say she had a collection of clay from every county in Ireland.'
Austin Flynn of Waterford, quoted in Brendan Fullam, *Hurling Giants* (1994).

'I'm Brian McEniff's wife and I just want to see the celebrations.'
Cautie McEniff, stopping off in the road on a certain Sunday in 1992.

'What about the baby? What about the baby?'
Man at a camogie match. For a time, married women were prevented from playing camogie, quoted in Brendan Fullam, *Legends of the Ash* (1997).

Lighter Side

Like great scores, some of the best GAA jokes weren't intended as jokes at all. There are also those moments of genius, in the memorable, pithy phrase that comes out in the spur of the moment, or the response to one of the organisation's many ludicrous situations, or the great saying of one of the games' many comedians who also happen to play, manage or follow. Long may they reign.

'I warned the boys they couldn't go through the league unbeaten and, unfortunately, they appear to have listened to me!'
Art McRory of Tyrone, after losing a league match.

'Everytime the Ó hAilpíns sit at table, it's a holocaust in the chicken world.'
Tom Humphries, *The Irish Times* (13 September 2003).

'When we entered the massage parlour the defendant was naked and in an aroused state. When asked the reason for his presence at the establishment, he said he was being treated for a GAA injury.'

The testimony of the arresting garda when the gardaí raided a massage parlor in Rathmines, quoted in the *Irish Independent.*

'Why was Mickey Cross when he saw what Johnny Dunne.'

Children's rhyme, from great encounter in 1933 All-Ireland, quoted in Brendan Fullam, *Hurling Giants* (1994).

'People slag me off about my right leg but without it I couldn't use my left.'

John Morley of Mayo.

'The GAA is still a world where you can ask a player if his family were GAA-oriented, and he will say yes, his uncle played for Galway, and you will ask what his name was, and he will say blankly, "Uncle Frank."'

Tom Humphries, *The Irish Times.*

'There was grand shhhckelping out there today.'

Páidí Ó Sé.

'As a group all players hang together or hang separately.'

Tom Mullaney, secretary of Roscommon county board.

'Mickey Joe made his championship debut in such a way that he will never be asked to make it again.'

John B. Keane.

'The night before I'd have three or four grand pints in the local pub, the safest place to be. And then on match day you'd go into the dressing room, the lads'd be banging the hurl off the table, they'd be psyching. I'd go in, tap the ball off the shower wall, get togged out and then go in and just have the last fag, meself and John Troy.'

Johnny Pilkington of Offaly, answering Mary Kennedy's question on how he prepared for a final on *Up for the Match*.

'Davey Forde wouldn't be a free-taker if you boiled him in a pot.'

Tom Ryan after the 1999 Munster final when Forde missed a tap-over free with 5 minutes to go.

'How would you play good football on a hurling pitch.'

Jack Conroy, Laois chairman, explaining how the county football team was beaten in Semple Stadium.

'I find it hard to see how my northern cousins could get so worked up about counties created by British imperialists.'

Colm O'Rourke, speaking on UTV's GAA show *End to End*.

Des Cahill: 'Did you have to explain to the English what hurling was all about?'

Dara Ó Briain, a former Wicklow hurler: 'No, but I have to explain it to the people of Wicklow.'

'You have stolen from God. It is not too late to repent. Turn up at Croke Park. Beg clemency. You will be spirited into Gowran where D.J. will receive you and offer you tea and talk to you for half an hour.'

Weblog, open letter to the guys who stole D.J. Carey's BMW.

'Roscommon may not have won any silverware this year, but they will be remembered for breaking one of the GAA's great taboos. Exactly what that taboo is, nobody will ever be quite sure, but they definitely smashed it.'

Keith Duggan, writing after the Roscommon players had a game of naked pool (20 July 2002).

'Leitrim for Croke Park, Mayo for Croagh Patrick.'

Sign outside a church in Leitrim after the 1994 Connacht championship.

'GAA nicknames are better: Sambo Hunter, Fat Larry, Babs, Bingo and so on.'

Weblog, 101 reasons why GAA is better than soccer.

'Attention Dubliners: Important notice arising out of the confusion that took place in Thurles the other Saturday, the grass verges outside the stadium may not be used for grazing ponies.'

Weblog, advice to Dublin GAA fans.

'What have Sinn Féin and Tyrone got in common? Sinn Féin have a better chance of seeing an All-Ireland.'

Colm O'Rourke, speaking before the 2003 All-Ireland final.

'If Micheál Martin had banned smoking in the workplace a few years back, Pilkington would have had to stand in the wind and the rain, in the beer garden outside the Offaly dressing room, for his last fag and he'd probably have caught a chill and wouldn't have been half the player he was.'

Mary Hannigan, (13 September 2004).

'In the evening Timmy McCarthy calls a meeting. There's been a problem. The hang sangwiches haven't arrived. We also have no training gear, no footballs. No holy water in a plastic bottle or other medical equipment. The two-litre bottles of Nash's fizzy orange we need to take to help us acclimatise are missing as well.'

Weblog, parody of Eamon Dunphy's biography of Roy Keane.

'A fireman asked me if the ball was safe.'

Roscommon player Jimmy Murray, after his pub was burned down and destroyed the football used in 1944 All-Ireland final.

'If you are a member of a certain political party and of the GAA, then you're shagged altogether.'

Charlie McCreevy, EU Commissioner and former Minister of Finance, speaking at the launch of TG4 series *Laochra Gael*, quoted in *The Irish Times* (2001).

'*The Meath Virus*: Throws you out of Windows.'

'*The Clare Virus*: Memory forgets everything before 1995.'

'*The Kerry Virus*: Five years of hard work wiped out by undetected Offaly mail.'

'*The Colin Lynch Virus*: Boots up some Waterford computers and carries on as if nothing happened.'

'*The Mick O'Dwyer Virus*: Attempts to install lots of foreign programs to replace existing slow-running applications.'

Weblog, GAA viruses.

'One night after Dublin lost to Kerry when myself and Páidí Lynch roamed around the capital and ended up in a Chinese.

There's a big commotion behind the kitchen. Some of the staff was shouting in Chinese and Páidí Lynch asks: what are they saying. I replied they are saying there's two of the worst feckin' Kerry footballers of all time. Let's get them out of here quick."'

Páidí Ó Sé.

'A farmer could make a tidy living in the amount of ground it takes Moss Keane to turn.'

Danny Lynch, GAA PRO.

'Reaching an All-Ireland final always brings a certain dread for any football fan, the fear of losing, the death of a dream, the frightful fall when the summit was so near being foremost. Yet probably the biggest dread of all is the prospect of a new county song being belted out day and night on the airwaves by some mutton-chopped country-and-western singer from the midlands. There's even some Mayomen who pray they'll never reach an All-Ireland final again. Not because the pain of the successive defeats in '96 and '97 was too much to stomach. No, because listening to Sam Maguire's "Coming Home to Mayo" to the air of the "Banana Boat Song" every minute of the day on Mid-West Radio was even worse. "May-Oh! Maaaaay-oh! Sam Maguire's coming home to Mayo!" It never ceases to amaze how Ireland, once the land of the haunting melody, a country that produced such beautiful ballads in olden times, could go so far astray in the art of penning a nice county tune.'

Sheepstealers.com, the Roscommon fans' website.

Literary Lions

The GAA has had a literary wing from the earliest days. *The Gael*, the first official newspaper of the association was as devoted to the promotion of literature as it was of Gaelic games, with Fenian leader John O'Leary being appointed as literary editor. Among the unknown poets whose work he published were W.B. Yeats, Douglas Hyde, Thomas William Rolleston and his sister Ellen O'Leary. The GAA's impact on Irish life is best seen in the way it infused itself into the literary tradition – Yeats and Joyce were contributors to early GAA journals – and there are also references in the work of more modern, rural writers, Patrick Kavanagh the foremost amongst them.

'Methinks I see this hurly all on foot.'

William Shakespeare, *The Life and Death of King John, Act* IV (1596).

'On the smooth plain of every true hurling/At dancing, sporting, racing or diversion.'

Brian Merriman, 'Cúirt an Mheán Oíche' (1780).

'I heard again the singing clash of ash, felt the horsehide ball firm in my grasp, sensed the thrill of swinging with the flying leather, smelt the green sod firm beneath studded feet. In a flash all these little things that I had cast one side were back with all their old appeal. That moment though was fatal, for one memory called up a host of others. Memories of sunshine on crowded stands in Croke Park, throngs along the touch-line, cheers that echoed and re-echoed as we, heroes for an hour, marched behind the swirling pipers and their throbbing drums. Memories of Thurles on some warm Sunday in July. Happy thousands there from every county in Munster.'

Pádraig Puirséil, *Hanrahan's Daughter* (1953).

'Kavanagh was not safe and needs a lot of practice and shows little judgement.'

Dundalk Democrat comment on the Inniskeen goalkeeper (August 1931).

'There was a rugby pitch on the grounds of the huge Gaelic football and hurling stadium of Croke Park, separated from it by a concrete wall, at the bottom of our street.'

Brendan Behan, *Borstral Boy* (1958).

'Old men, children, middle-aged men who used to be foot-ballers and now played only in their imaginations and their talk, went up to Canada Cross to surround the victorious footballers, slap them on the back, inquire about the great moments of glory and who made them in the winning of the victory. And the women came too, the women who hated the football because it maimed their men, sapped their energy, usurped the love of their men, but who later learned to take their own pleasure in the victories of their men, though it sometimes mean their own loss. All traffic was stopped around the crossroads. The lazy, summer afternoon in the small town exploded.'

William Cotter Murray, *Michael Joe* (1965).

'All sporting subjects are superficial. The emotion is a momentary puff of gas.'

Patrick Kavanagh, 'Gut Yer Man', an essay on Gaelic football, in the monthly literary magazine *Envoy* (1950).

'"Why do you refuse to talk about Kavanagh? Is he not the man who put your village on the map?" One of the wise men slowly lifted his head looked the professor in the eye and said, "Kavanagh cost us a county final."'

Augustine Martin. The village of Iniskeen was a couple of points ahead of Latton in the 1930 County final when Patrick Kavanagh, the keeper, seeing the ball at the other end of the field, sauntered over to the sideline to buy a bottle of orange. By the time he made it back, the ball was in the net and the game was lost. Later Kavanagh would claim, though possibly apocryphally, that he had wandered off to buy an ice cream.

'Rugby is a game for barbarians played by gentlemen. Football is a game for gentlemen played by barbarians.'

Oscar Wilde.

'Gaelic is a game for barbarians played by barbarians.'

Jacques Smith, rugby journalist, making an addendum to Wilde.

Managers, Coaches and Motivation

The pre-match speech is one of the secrets of the GAA. We have no records of many of the greatest speeches because the select few who heard them kept them to themselves. In recent years, managers have become more forthcoming with their own after-match conferences and, oh joy, a capacity to get a little too relaxed when giving an interview to local radio.

'Think of your fathers, think of your grandfathers, think of the men that died lads. Jaysus lads, the men that died so that you could get out there with a stick and a small ball to puck around. So get out there lads and let every blow lead to a feckin' funeral. Don't be afraid to break hurleys lads – there's plenty of hurleys on the sideline – hit 'em hard, they're no re-lation. I don't want to see ye coming back in here with dirty jerseys, I want to see ye with blood-stained jerseys, so get out now boys and enjoy yerselves.'

Jon Kenny, as *D'Unbelievables* manager, Jimmy Ryan, some players claim he wasn't exaggerating that much.

'You know what pain is? Pain is coming out of Croke Park after losing the All-Ireland! With your f***ing head down on the ground after being beaten by Offaly in an All-Ireland final! That's what pain is.'

Ger Loughnane (attrib.).

'In 1940 I was part of a Limerick team that defeated Kilkenny in the All-Ireland final. I wouldn't have believed then that it would take so long for Limerick to return again to Croke Park for All-Ireland day. I was a young man then but I amn't a young man now. Go out and win it.'

Jackie Power, pep talk in the dressing room before Limerick beat Kilkenny to win the 1973 All-Ireland final.

'A bit of a ditch shouldn't make that much difference between Laois and Kilkenny.'

Georgie Leahy, half-time speech at a Laois–Kilkenny match (1984).

'We have no more than a 50–50 chance.'

Pat Spillane, before Kerry's 1977 Munster championship first round match against Tipperary.

'Now listen lads, I'm not happy with our tackling. We're hurting them, but they keep getting up.'

John B. Keane.

'There is no getting away from it, if you want to do well, it takes a lot of time. It's not just about training. It's about the preparation that goes into your training and your interaction with individuals within the team. The players have lives to live as well. You have to try and accommodate them any way you can. It takes time to think about that and explore things with players. It's not just a football business, it's a people business.'

Mickey Harte, Tyrone's 2003 All-Ireland winning manager.

'Now lads, you're going out today to play the best team that ever wore jerseys. You're fit and well. So are they. The game will be won in the last quarter of an hour. They will be tired. So will you. The man with the greater willpower will win. Let it be the Tipperary men.'

Tom Semple, speaking before the 1937 Munster final, quoted by Jimmy Butler Coffey of Tipperary in Brendan Fullam, *Hurling Giants* (1994).

'The big thing nowadays is to win, win, win, regardless of what county you manage. It's no good, when you come into a job, setting a goal of building the team up so that we can be in such a position in two years. You have to be seen to win. That pressure is always there and county boards are nearly as bad as supporters in looking for it.'

Brian Talty, former Galway player.

'Wexford have given their best, we have them now.'

Paddy Grace of Kilkenny, speaking at half-time during a Leinster hurling championship match between Wexford and Kilkenny. Wexford were 8 points up at the time. Kilkenny won.

'There is a clear division between those counties who pay their managers and those who don't. It used to be that counties who appointed a man from within the county did not pay anything other than official GAA expenses while if outsiders were brought in they got paid. But then, when the word got out about how much some of the outside managers were allegedly getting, it was inevitable that some of those managers from inside the counties began to demand a fee as well. All these payments are done outside official GAA structures which means that, as far as county chairmen and other high GAA officials are concerned, they don't take place at all. That enables these people to assure the public their manager is only getting the official mileage rate, the same as the players. But getting around rules is a way of life in the GAA and there are always kind people, who are not elected GAA officials, to make sure the financial deal hammered out with the manager is carried out.'

Eugene McGee, *Irish Independent* (20 September 2002).

'Every year we had a different trainer. We had more trainers than Sheikh Mohammad.'

Pat Mangan of Kildare.

'While there were claims that managers were being paid under the table, the GAA couldn't even find the tables.'

Peter Quinn, former GAA president.

'You say that there is no way an injured player could possibly play even though you are certain he will. Alternatively, you deny you have any injury worries while knowing that two star players are unlikely to play. The most blatant form of this style of course is publishing an incorrect team. All the "great" managers do this nowadays and many of them seem to actually think that the media and the public believe the teams they publish. They do not seem to realise that they are merely making fools of themselves and more often confusing their own team rather than their opponents. Young managers should avoid this style in the interest of their own self-respect.'

Eugene McGee, *Irish Independent* (13 January 2003).

'The best psychology is common sense. If we can come up with enough of that and apply it, we'll all be happy boys on Sunday evening.'

Gerald McCarthy, former Cork manager.

'Everybody in the county needs to move away from the culture of blame and easy short-sighted solutions like the scapegoating and finger-pointing that have existed right up to the present day.'

Paddy Carr, on quitting as manager of Louth.

'Anybody starting off their own business, working for an employer or repping, definitely wouldn't have time to manage a football team at the moment.'

Martin McHugh, former Cavan manager.

'Whenever a team loses, there's always a row at half-time but when they win, it's an inspirational speech.'

John O'Mahony, Galway manager.

'By the time I got to the Red Cow Roundabout, I was an hour on the road. By the time I got through it, it was nearly another hour. If I'd taken the job, it would have taken me two and a half hours to get there — and that's with a good run through the traffic. Then you'd have training for an hour and a half and after that you'd be hanging around for another hour. Throw in two hours to drive home afterwards and at the end of it all, you'd nearly have put in an eight-hour shift. It would have been a job on top of your job.'

Brian Talty, on why he turned down the Offaly job (2004).

'The smallest thing can turn a big match and I just think a few bad decisions went against us at crucial moments.'

Eugene McGee, compiling a list of ready-made quotations for losing team managers (13 January 2003).

Jim 'Tough' Barry

'Cork are like mushrooms, they can come overnight.'
Jim Barry.

'Jim Barry had a tremendous ability to bring out the best in the team he was training. When the training session started he used to go down to the park, as we used to call it, it's Páirc Uí Chaoimh now, to make sure that the grass was cut. If it wasn't, he'd kick up holy murder. He'd make sure that the jerseys were washed and the towels were washed. If somebody was working, maybe it was shift work, Jim would go to the boss, the managing director and insisted he be let off. After matches, win or lose, he always made sure the team was sitting down to a good meal. He wouldn't let anyone interfere with the welfare of the team in any respect. Jim was generous He didn't have a lot of money but he made what little he had available to the people who were in trouble from time to time.'

Jack Lynch, quoted in Colm Keane, *Hurling's Top Twenty* (2002).

Jimmy Barry Murphy

'Jimmy Barry Murphy. My three favourite footballers.'
Cork boy, after the 1973 All-Ireland final.

'I'm Kilbarron's third most famous person.'
Jimmy Barry Murphy.

'May his greyhounds never get left in the traps.'
Enda McEvoy, *Sunday Tribune*.

Seán Boylan

'I wonder if Meath had scored goals like that would they have been allowed.'
Seán Boylan, after a 2002 Dublin–Meath match.

'There's affinity between men who go out and have a drink together that people like me will never be part of it… I used to talk to lads in the pub and they'd be complaining about something and I'd go away and get it fixed and I'd meet them again and say, "Hey, I got that fixed up", and they'd say, "What?" Looking at me as if I had ten heads. It was just talk, their chance to get things off their own chest. I was intruding.'
Seán Boylan.

'Perception is everything when you are a manager. You have to appear to the world at large to be a very co-operative person, always willing to talk to the media and sounding so sincere that everybody who reads your words will believe them. Your model should be Seán Boylan of Meath and you could do worse than spend a day in The National Library studying the utterances of Seán in those years when Meath were winning All-Irelands. His comments will show you how you can remain popular, always be believed and yet never say anything that gives away any of the real secrets of how you carry out your football business.'

Eugene McGee, *Irish Independent* (13 January 2003).

'Sometimes, I'll look at the lads and I'll know what I planned for them is all wrong. I'll just tear it up in my head and start again.'

Seán Boylan.

'It seems crazy. There are nights when snow might be coming down or sheets of rain or whatever and you'd wonder about it all but I'd always be glad when I got there that I had gone. I'd get something out of it always.'

Seán Boylan.

Eamonn Cregan

'He ate the s***e out of us.'

An Offaly player, on one of Eamonn Cregan's half-time speeches.

'He's fantastic at half-time. I've seen our team down five or six points at half-time and Eamonn would give a fantastic speech, motivate the players. He knows his football and he gets that across to players, they have complete confidence in him.'

Seán McGahern.

'If they get a sniff of it once, they'll always want it. It's only a small part of the overall setup, but it's a very positive part of it.'

Eamonn Cregan, on underage victory.

'I do get frustrated when I see a player going for the ball, knowing what he should do, knowing what I would have done – and he doesn't do it. Now with players I keep it very simple, try not to complicate things. Explain the fault to the player and get him to go away and improve on the skill.'

Eamonn Cregan.

Brian Cody

'He's a man that stays in the background in a lot of ways, but says what has to be said and doesn't make easy decisions.'

D.J. Carey, on Brian Cody.

Cyril Farrell

'Offaly can play hurling wisely and economically; Cork cannot. Why? Because for more than a little while now, especially but not exclusively up front, Cork have been sliding, declining, into the soloing and handpassing methodology the Cyril Farrell system. That thing is a truncation and a desecration as who should ordain that Mozart be played with bodhráns and tin whistles, and all the soaring and transcendent expressions and potentialities be discarded.'

Kevin Cashman, *Sunday Independent.*

Liam Griffin

'Griffin dealt with it the way you'd deal with a young horse terrified by a white bag on the road. You wouldn't push the horse – you'd gently cajole and find a way for the horse to believe that it was his idea to go past.'

Niamh Fitzpatrick, the Wexford sports psychologist.

'Liam Griffin had built us up so much we thought we could nearly fly.'

Martin Storey.

Kevin Heffernan

'Winning is a physical pleasure, but as a player – as a manager, it's a more cerebral business. Can you beat him tactically or intellectually? It's in there you get a little buzz.'

Kevin Heffernan.

'He reinvented the way Gaelic football was played. Twice.'

Tom Humphries, *The Irish Times.*

'I didn't mind a fella who wanted to know why or to argue the toss. That was good. He had to understand, though. In the end we'd do it my way.'

Kevin Heffernan.

'Getting in their heads. That's what the game is about. It's an extremely important part to be sure. Get them on the right wavelength, the same wavelength. What we went through together was deeper than just football. We'd be concerned about each other. Concerned about anything which would perturb a player.'

Kevin Heffernan.

'The thing you had to be afraid of with Heffernan was the arm around the shoulder. In thirty seconds he could convince you that you weren't right for a game. You'd be killing yourself in training and then you'd be almost grateful he was dropping you.'

Dave Billings.

Michael Babs Keating

'Sheep in a heap.'

Michael Keating, describing Offaly in 1998, before he departed as team manager in mid-season.

'That was sh**e, lads. I don't know where ye get yere standards from, but I can tell ye that sh**e is not good enough for Tipperary.'

Michael Keating, half-time speech (1987).

'Good hurlers playing the game the way it should be played.'

Michael Keating, on his dream team.

'It was the saddest of sad curtains for Michael Keating. For nigh on eight years, he ceaselessly strove to instill rhythm and harmony and brio into the hurling of his charges, and just as ceaselessly demanded that they evince those properties on the field of play. It is little wonder that the good folk of Tipperary never found the grace in their hearts to give Michael Keating the credit and deification that the rest of the nation accords Jack Charlton for achieving less.'

Kevin Cashman, *Sunday Independent* (5 June 1994).

'Tipperary would be disappointed if they didn't win the 2002 Munster final by ten points.'

Michael Keating.

'A message in every ball.'

Michael Keating's advice to teams.

Philip 'Fan' Larkin

'Everybody else tells him about the scores he gets, I remind him about the ones he missed.'

Fan Larkin, Kilkenny minor team manager, on Henry Shefflin (1997).

Ger Loughnane

'Hurling is the bain of my life.'

Ger Loughnane, after the 1995 national hurling league final defeat.

'As a Clare minor my first introduction was under the late Paddy Duggan, who gave a most amazing speech in the dressing room in Limerick. While whacking a hurley off a table and as his false teeth did three laps of his mouth, he called on the team to kill and maim the opposition, before saying an Our Father and three Hail Marys.'

Ger Loughnane.

'The first thing I would do is purchase a gun and leave it to my wife at home. Because if I ever insinuate that I'm return-ing to county management, then I will tell her to have me shot straight away. It's something you should do once and once only.'

Ger Loughnane.

'There is no better way of firing up your own team, especially if they are beginning to lag, or get smug or over-confident in themselves, than to have a bit of controversy or create a situation where people think everybody is against them.'

Ger Loughnane, quoted in John Scally, *Raising the Banner* (2001).

'There's not a minute in the day I don't think about hurling.'

Ger Loughnane, talking to fellow selector Tony Considine.

'Everybody asks the question, What changed Clare from losers into winners? And you can't look beyond Ger Loughnane for it. Loughnane put confidence into them and a fanatical will to win. Even allowing for the very talented group that he had, without Loughnane we would never have won.'

Jimmy Smyth.

'In his message to the hurlers – and to the non-combatants, too – of Clare, Loughnane was the resurrection of Jim Larkin; and is now just as immortal. The great are great only because we are on our knees. Let us arise. Of course, that is not to suggest that these men were of equal stature. For one thing, Loughnane could never concede parity of esteem to forwards. That diminished him and, in the end, undid him. Fine forward lines are assembled and melded – not spilt out of a lucky bag.'

Kevin Cashman, *Sunday Independent.*

'In a purely hurling context Ger is a dog. But a dog was exactly what we needed here, and what we'd never had before. Traditionally Clare were always too nice.'

Clare hurler.

'Ger Loughnane is the kind of man who can euphemise fanaticism as common sense, who can disguise obsession as the only sensible way to behave.'

John Scally, *Raising the Banner* (2001).

'Why were Clare so hyped up for the second game? After all, we've played in All-Ireland finals, in All-Ireland semi-finals, we've played against Tipperary in the Munster final when the tension was even higher. Why were Clare so hyped up? The key to that is the last sentence of the referee's report of the first game: "Gerald McCarthy, Waterford, came on to the field and abused the umpire and myself and I booked him." Not alone did Gerald abuse the referee and umpire, but he continually abused Clare players.'

Ger Loughnane, speaking on Clare FM (6 August 1998).

'You could actually see the improvement brought about by Ger's coaching on the training field in the weeks coming up to the match.'

Cyril Lyons.

'Nobody gives better quotes or better value than Ger Loughnane.'

Tom Humphries, *The Irish Times*.

Justin McCarthy

'They are lovely terms of speech – tactics and gameplan – but hurling is a game of reaction. You can ask players to perform certain roles, but they have to be able to react quickly. For instance, you can tell a back to go out in front of his man, but if the ball goes over his head, he has to react to that. You can't plan for a goal like Joe Deane scored against Clare or Paul Flynn's against Limerick.'

Justin McCarthy.

'Hurling is too serious a game to be dabbling with. I want to get action. I like to see the game expanding. I don't want to see it being controlled by two or three teams. I believe you can achieve things with the right application and the right attitude. Tradition is a killer disease within the GAA, it's an awful thing to get over. To give people the belief to over-come, that is a big job. Coming from a strong county where we were reared on success, I can transfer that knowledge easier.'

Justin McCarthy.

Brian McEniff

'If you take the team average of three evenings a week plus a match and all the ancillary work that goes in which is never seen, any sort of county manager is talking of [putting in] 30 to 35 hours per week. You are dealing with a panel of 30 players now, so it's like a wee industry in its own right. On top of that, you have doctors, physios, masseurs and a county board to deal with. Then there are other factors no one thinks about – the pressure on your home life and the stress involved in the job.'

Brian McEniff.

'He's just a GAA man, pure and simple. But a very streetwise GAA man.'

Pádraig MacShea, former Donegal captain, on Brian McEniff.

'In his eyes, it was as if the world had ended with that final whistle. You couldn't talk to him he was so down. Donegal just hadn't performed. They'd been beaten by a mediocre Galway team. And he couldn't bear the thought of that.'

Pádraig MacShea, former Donegal captain, on McEniff's reaction to the 1983 All-Ireland semi-final.

John Maughan

'Of course it was disappointing to lose those All-Ireland finals but I still got up the next day and carried on. I still had a life to lead. I love football, I don't just like it. You can't just like it.'

John Maughan.

'I can't guarantee you we'll win, but I guarantee you this, we won't be walked on.'

John Maughan, talking before the 1996 All-Ireland final.

'Unlike Griffin, he is more of a pragmatist and will settle for tomorrow being the Jurys Cabaret of Sport rather than the *Riverdance*, as long as Mayo win.'

Seán Moran, on John Maughan.

Billy Morgan

'Billy Morgan poured his heart and soul into every team. He got hot under the collar easily, he ranted and raved at re-erees, opposing players and officials. He fell out with his own players, but cared deeply about their well being.'

Colm O'Rourke (29 February 2004).

Mick O'Dwyer

'You don't ask Mick O'Dwyer for a comment, you just wait for him to make it.'

Ian O'Riordan, *The Irish Times*.

'Croke Park have never consulted me about anything. They would be afraid because they consider me a bit of a radical.'

Mick O'Dwyer, talking on Radio Kerry (December 2000).

'I'm not going to even think about the northern systems or what way they prepare their teams. I have no intention of doing that good, bad or indifferent. I'm going to prepare a team my way and I'm not too worried about their systems in the north at all, I can assure you.'

Mick O'Dwyer (February 2004).

'He'll be training my young lads yet.'

Eoin Liston, on Mick O'Dwyer.

Donal O'Grady

'This is it lads. This is tough going now. We're going bad. But this is it. This is Munster championship. It's tough. It's hard-nose. These are the situations. There's no need for panic.'

Donal O'Grady.

'There's loads of trainers in the GAA, but very few coaches. Everybody knows what you're meant to do, but how do you do it?'

Donal O'Grady.

'For Donal O'Grady training at seven means seven on the pitch. If you're late, he'll warn you and he'll let you know he can get someone else who'll come at seven. After the first incident you just tell yourself you'll never be late again. With other managers it was always "lads you're good enough, go out and do it". With Donal we analyse the opposition, what they've got, what they do. This that and the other. He runs the shop like a school. Abide by the rules. If you don't like it move to a new school. This year, well it's hard for us older lads to grasp. We're not used to it. We're used to taking it seriously on the pitch but being late for training or having a bit of crack, if you're chatting when you are stretching it's "lads I hear you talking, you're not focused lads". It wouldn't be popular but it's gotten results.'

Seán Óg Ó hAilpín.

Páidí Ó Sé

'Páidí Ó Sé is buttoned up like the most devout girl in the Amish community when it came to the pre-final interview.'

Tom Humphries, *Laptop Dancing and the Nanny-Goat Mambo* (2003).

'I have my own new ideas for the team in the New Year. I want to bring in a bit of creativity. I believe there needs to be a new freshness there but then again I'm not going to divulge any of that publicly. I don't want any of the country to know what I'm doing.'

Páidí Ó Sé, *Sunday Independent* (5 January 2003).

'One time, before leading the team out to Croke Park, he hopped the ball so hard off the ground that it made smithereens of an overhead light. He'd be shouting and running up the walls and jumping. He'd hit the ceiling. He'd be on one side of the room and the quieter lads would be at the other. But what a motivator and what a player.'

Mick O'Dwyer.

'He threw his bag into the same corner of the dressing room where he sat, stripped off and put on his runners. Sometimes he'd think to put on a pair of shorts, other times he'd be buck naked, running around the dressing room. Then he'd let this roar out of him, like a massive release. We'd be looking at each other, thinking to ourselves "he's finally gone crazy".'

Jack O'Shea, on Páidí Ó Se.

'Just when you think you've cracked it, football will give you a kick up the backside… When Oisín McConville cut inside and fired that goal to the net in the second half, the x-factor was unleashed upon us. A 100 years of oppression, of f***ing helicopters, of jack-booted troops kicking them when they were down – the lot.'

Páidí Ó Sé (28 September 2002).

'It's better as a player but when you are 44 and two stone overweight and going slow, winning one as a manager isn't bad.'

Páidí Ó Sé (1997).

'I think Páidí Ó Sé is getting slightly carried away about his own importance. Ogie Moran got a hard time after losing a Munster final and Mickey O'Sullivan was torn to shreds when Clare beat us in a Munster final back in 1992. So Páidí would want to remember that we were beaten by Armagh, and in my eyes Armagh were handed the All-Ireland and, because Armagh won it, it was suddenly okay to lose it.'

Ger Power, talking on Radio Kerry (January 2003).

'It might take the Kerry public a while to appreciate him, but I think history will be kind to Páidí. It was never just about football with him.'

Dara Ó Cinneide, on Páidí Ó Sé.

Jackie Power

'Sometimes you had to wonder were we playing for Power rather than for Limerick. We felt we had to give a little more because it was Jackie.'

Ned Rea, on Jackie Power.

And back to Jimmy Ryan

'Ye're sitting there thinking, "Jimmy Ryan is too hard on us." Well I tell you something, I'm not, ye'll know all about it next year when ye're playing under-14.'

Jon Kenny, *D'Unbelievables*.

More than a Game

After the Troubles in Northern Ireland began in 1968, the ideological background that the GAA had carried from its foundation in 1884 was challenged. To this day, it has few adherents among the northern unionist community, and has only been partially successful in extending its appeal beyond the rural heartlands which have provided most of its successful teams in both codes.

'We don't play Gaelic football.'
John Taylor, UUP minister (August 1996).

'The Association shall actively support the Irish language, traditional Irish dancing, music, song and other aspects of Irish culture.'
Article 4 of the GAA.

'The GAA was founded to check a grave racial menace in the deterioration of the pastimes of the people through want of organised control, and to combat the influence of other games and customs which threatened to destroy the surviving cultural inheritances of the Gael.'

Introduction to *The GAA Rule Book*.

'The Association shall be non-party political and no committee, club, council or representative thereof shall take part as such in any party political movement.'

Rule 8 of the GAA.

'People say the GAA is a monocultural organisation. It is more like an agricultural organisation.'

Jack Boothman, former GAA president (2005).

'Coming up to All-Ireland time, the annual spate of agricultural photographs of the finalists began to appear. The All-Ireland star is pictured in wellington boots turned down over the tops, wearing dungarees over a striped collarless shirt, a cap on the back of his head, and a trawneen of grass stuck in his mouth. He is being handed a mug of tea in the haggard by an equally agricultural looking girl. The caption generally reads: "As he puts the finishing touches to his hayrick, our Croke Park stalwart is offered a welcome mug of tea by Mary Ann."'

J.P. Murray.

'When the twentieth century dawned, the Gaelic Athletic Association could look back on 15 years of effort and achievement, the Gaelic League on seven. Two hundred years earlier Ireland, in the brief period of 15 months, had experienced Briseadh na Boinne, Aughrim's great disaster and the flight of the Wild Geese that followed the Treaty of

Limerick. During the two intervening centuries her alien rules belittled and ignored the customs and language, the games and pastimes of the hidden Ireland. The GAA and the league combined to reawaken legitimate pride of race, to raise the ideal of nationhood, and concept above and beyond party and class. A good beginning had been made, but much remained to be done.'

Pádraig Purséil.

'One of the most important and original mass movements of its day, its importance has not yet been recognised.'

Conor Cruise O'Brien, polemicist and politician, commenting on the GAA in a Thomas Davis lecture, The Shaping of Modern Ireland (1956).

'The GAA might have turned into a sports organisation and nothing else. The extraordinary growth of this one humble enough association is really a measure of the vitality that lies inert in the common people. In spirit as in its achievement the GAA is not only unique but astonishing.'

Daniel Corkery, historian.

'The GAA is a national trust, an entity which we feel we hold in common ownership. It is there to administer to our shared passion. It was like a lifebuoy and we clung on doggedly. Anything the GAA got it got for itself.'

Tom Humphries, The Irish Times.

'The ideal, ambition, resolve of the GAA's founders was to bring recreation, health, self-reliance and communal pride to the cosmhuintir; in defiance of the usurpers and racists and their toadies and flunkies who monopolised and misgoverned every brand and branch of organised sport in the land. What the GAA's founders achieved is self-evident. But the methods and manner of the achievement the native genius and spirit of the meitheal: co-operation, service, voluntarism ah! there are pages to be torn from the history books and obliterated, if the new and better GAA is to be moulded in the image of the successors of Cusack and Davin.'

Kevin Cashman, *Sunday Independent.*

'When it comes to the GAA, one lot genuinely doesn't know what makes the other lot tick. A sport that crosses all classes, drawn on local talent with the strongest local support, is enviable in Protestant eyes. Theirs is a thinner sense of community, the Orange Hall a local hub for only one section, the fierce allegiance of GAA fans is a major mystification for Protestant onlookers.'

Fionnuala O'Connor, Northern Irish writer (2001).

'After captaining Kerry to All-Ireland victory in 1929, Joe Barrett handed over the next captaincy in 1931 to Captain Con Brosnan, a Free State Army officer, who was a member of the army which had incarcerated Barrett in various locations for almost a year-and-a-half.'

J.J. Barrett.

'The GAA, after all, is not just a sporting organisation. It is a cultural entity as well. It has visions of itself and of Ireland, and those visions are, generally speaking, ones which many people would share, of a united Ireland at peace, playing Irish sports, indulging in Irish pastimes, and daily celebrating Irish culture free of foreign influence. In many senses, they are what are known in the US as family values. Only the darkest-dyed anti-Irish bigot would argue that such aspirations are wrong or frivolous or banal. They are not. They are profoundly worthy.'

Kevin Myers, *The Irish Times* (11 June 1998).

'The GAA was founded to be, and remains, a benevolent society in the truest sense of that term: it exists to promote communal well-being.'

Kevin Cashman, *Sunday Independent.*

'The mission of the GAA is to make men Gaelic in heart and spirit, to work for the advancement of their country's welfare, and to band Irishmen in one great brotherhood actuated by a worthy and noble purpose.'

Munster Express (26 March 1927).

'Were it not for the GAA when it stood for Ireland, England in her great war would have annexed much of her finest bone and muscle that was saved for Ireland.'

Michael Collins, speaking before Leinster hurling final (11 September 1921).

'If ever our national games should die, then in truth it may be said that *Knocknagow* would be no more.'

Rev J.M. Hayes, founder of Muintir na Tire (1943).

'When William Webb-Ellis was but a young cove at Rugby school, one day he picked the ball up and ran with it. A Tipperary friend assures me that when asked why he had so flagrantly broken the rules of football, he replied, "Because that's the way we play it at home, Sir." Home for the Webb-Ellises, my Tipperary friend assures me, was Nenagh. Nenagh – or rugby, as it is improperly known – was the sport of the middle-class urban types; very British army, either unionist or apolitical. Gaelic was for the nationally minded rural lads who would no more play rugby (because, of course, they didn't know it was in fact Nenagh) than they would sing "God Save the Queen".'

Kevin Myers, *The Irish Times* (29 January 2000).

'Too often we see the players wriggling and shifting during it, or standing with bored, hangdog expressions, or with heads down, only to burst into activity when the crowd starts to roar, long before the last notes are finished.'

Letter to *The Irish Times*, on the singing of 'Amhrán na bhFíann' (12 September 2001).

'The GAA is unwittingly giving aid and comfort to those who view the GAA as the IRA at play and believe club officials are legitimate targets.'

Steven King, Ulster Unionist activist, *The Irish Times* (12 October 1998).

'The largest sporting organisation in Ireland, the GAA, voted to support the terror campaign.'

Kevin Myers, *The Irish Times* (15 January 2003).

'Kevin Myers', Irish Times columnist, remarks which appear to insinuate some kind of institutional link between the Gaelic Athletic Association and the IRA, are malicious, misguided and deeply hurtful to all members of the GAA. Contrary to Mr Myers' insinuation, at no point did the GAA vote to support the terror campaign or indeed any other terror campaign.'

Letter to *The Irish Times* (18 January 2003).

'This is not an abstract issue. Over the past 30 years, a number of officials and players have been murdered by loyalist paramilitaries because of their association with the GAA. Other people have been murdered for the crime of standing outside a GAA clubhouse. Club premises have been the target of bomb and arson attacks. The paramilitary organisations involved tried to justify these actions by allegations of GAA support for the IRA.'

Letter to *The Irish Times* (20 January 2003).

'An apology. Here it is. It wasn't 30 years, but more like 24, and I apologise for that.'

Kevin Myers, *The Irish Times* (22 January 2003).

'Between 1994 and 2002 there were 594 attacks on symbolic properties such as churches, chapels, Orange Halls and GAA clubs, an average of five attacks a month over a nine-year period.'

Neil Jarman, Institute for Conflict Research.

'What if the GAA presented a bill for the social work it has done since 1884, the gaps it's filled, the culture it has preserved, the facilities it has provided, the sense of identity it has helped this country foster?'

Tom Humphries, *The Irish Times* (14 April 2003).

'The Gaelic Athletic Association is a great sporting organisation. It has contributed hugely to community identity and solidarity. It has knit together small rural villages and deprived urban areas; helped to merge them into local, county and regional organisations and given spectators a range of wonderful games to shout about. Its voluntary nature has attracted ordinary citizens as administrators, coaches and committed supporters. Most importantly, it has provided leadership and good quality sporting facilities for an enormous number of young men and women on this island. And now it is being asked to behave as a healing force in Northern Ireland.'

Irish Times editorial (8 November 2001).

'Kerry was at the core of Civil War atrocities and, being a heartland of Gaelic football, crucially central to the healing which the game helped to bring to a bitterly divided people.'

Paddy Downey.

'"Amhrán na bhFíann" is not a national anthem.'

Con Houlihan, in a letter to *The Irish Times* (February 1997).

'You are not politicians, but patriots working to bring back the things that were characteristic of the ancient civilisation of our country, our glorious old language, our music, our dances, our games.'

Cardinal MacRory, speaking to GAA members at a function in St Mary's Hall, Belfast (1 January 1928).

'Our Gaelic pastimes are becoming more popular with all classes of public. It is no longer vulgar to witness Gaelic games on Sundays. Our Gaelic Games are the sports of the poor. On the walls of the mud-wall cabins hang the jerseys of the Gael. In the corner by the fireside hangs the hurley by the light of the house. These football jerseys may not be coloured with refined taste, this hurley may be but rudely daubed, yet this jersey covers a rough – not coarse – and manly breast and no effeminate arms dare swing that old huricy. While these our Gaelic Games continue to be the pastimes of the poor, so long will an insuperable barrier be placed between our manly race and decadence.'

Patrick Ramsbottom (Thigeen Roe), *Leinster Leader* (1906).

'Sporting and cultural bodies should shape their policies to help end the political and religious division and, eventually, the border. The GAA, for instance, should be very careful not to behave in the six counties as an organisation for Catholics only. Without abandoning any of its nationalism or gaelicism, the GAA should try to induce thousands to Protestants to watch their games and eventually play them. Therefore Catholic hymns should neither be played nor sung before or after football and hurling matches. The national anthem, "Amhrán na bhFiann", should not be played on such occasions in the six counties, not should the major games be played on Sundays.'

Briseadh na Teorann by Eaarnan de Blaghd, translated and quoted by Breandán Ó hEithir, *Over the Bar* (1984).

'How is [an Orange Order member in Northern Ireland] expected to react when he sees a GAA cavalcade tearing through his village playing republican songs and flying Tricolours, yet he has been told his little church parade is liable to be rerouted at the behest of a bogus residents' group?'

Ruth Dudley Edwards, Orange Order activist and historian, *The Irish Times* (30 June 1998).

'The GAA caters for 14,050 youth teams and 5,833 adult teams in its clubs and has a playing population of nearly half-a-million people. It has provided sporting and social facilities in virtually every town and parish in Ireland, urban and rural. It has also provided an infrastructure for many of the great occasions that adorn our annual sporting calendar. In doing this for 119 years the GAA through its members and their support has spent billions of euro and successfully promoted its games which have provided a healthy sporting and social outlet for generations of our young people and a sporting focus for the enjoyment and benefit of the population generally. The GAA has done this on a voluntary and non-profit basis. The direct benefit that has accrued to the Exchequer far exceeds any financial assistance that the association ever received.'

Danny Lynch, GAA PRO (12 March 2002).

'Antrim County Board have a chequered history in relation to boycotts. Essentially the Antrim Board's policy has been, well, how should I put it… to boycott boycotts. And I just don't know how they're going to get around this one.'

Letter to the *Andersonstown News* (December 2004).

'When Derry won the All-Ireland we displayed in plain bright colours one of the most interesting but little remarked-on aspects of life in the North: that while the objective statistics confirm that Catholics, in general, are worse off than Protestants, it's also true that, in general, Catholics have more crack. It's more fun being a Fenian.'

Eamonn McCann, BBC radio (September 1993).

'Ireland has no chance of Olympic champions when the GAA is openly referred to as the main sport in Ireland. It is up to the media to show the children of Ireland that many more sports exist outside their village or county.'

Letter to *The Irish Times* (1 November 2000).

'Gaels, do not be supporters of betting. Do not even allow the habit of "I'll bet you" to grow on you. There may, apparently, be little in it, but much may come out of it.'

Michael Cusack, in the oldest-surviving edition of *The Celtic Times* (19 February 1887).

'The GAA is the Catholic equivalent of the Orange Order.'

Harold McCusker, unionist MP, quoted in Breandán Ó hEithir, *Over the Bar* (1984).

'Now is the time for him to present the GAA's nabobs with an offer they can't refuse or a compulsory purchase order. Thereby allowing the GAA to get back to Thurles, to its ideals, to its roots, to its true nature, to its comity, to its service and simple goodness. For if that is not done the GAA faces revolution, or professionalism or extinction, which is the same thing as professionalism.'

Kevin Cashman, *Sunday Independent.*

National Leagues:
The Forgotten Competition?

They have been around since 1926, and for a time in the 1960s attracted attendances in excess of 70,000. But for much of their existence, the national leagues have been regarded as a poor wintry relation of the summer championships. It is easy to forget that some of the greatest games in GAA history were played in the winter.

'You get more contact in an old-time waltz at the old-folks' home than in a National League final.'
Pat Spillane, *The Sunday Game*.

'If Offaly win the National League again this year it will be the greatest accident since the *Titanic*.'
Paul O'Kelly of Offaly.

'Reaching the playoff stages is usually – but by no means always – a sign that team development is going well. You generally learn more from losing a match than winning one – defeated quarter-finalists can get the best of both worlds.'

Seán Moran, pointing out that the path to success usually involves losing a league quarter-final, *The Irish Times* (10 April 1999).

'Kerry must take the National League seriously. Too often they have used it as scaffolding for the All-Ireland. This is belittling what used to be a great competition and is unfair to those counties who take it seriously. And winning never does a team any harm.'

Con Houlihan, *Sunday World* (21 September 2003).

'The defining moment for the league was when it became all played in the one year, from February on. Previously any team that won the All-Ireland treated the early stages of the league like a lap of honour. After that it became more important as preparation for the championship.'

Nicky English, Tipperary manager.

'The bucolic little curiosity that is the National Hurling League resumes tomorrow in the half-light of an infant February. Underwhelmed and over-taxed, only the hard core will squeeze through turnstiles to see its latest incarnation. The league is a grey, long-winded rehearsal. Seven pounds in, several decades out of kilter.'

Vincent Hogan, *Irish Independent*.

Officials, Mentors and Administrators

The labyrinthine structure of the GAA, embracing 40 central committees and hundreds more representing provinces, counties and clubs, has created a bureaucracy as formidable as any thrown up by the public service. All these officials have conflicting agendas and aspirations, providing rich material for the verbal jousting in which the GAA excels.

'That crowd couldn't pick periwinkles.'
Paddy Bawn Brosnan, talking on the Kerry selectors after a heavy defeat.

'Anybody looking around the Congress Hall last Saturday could see three notable things: the number of men aged 50 or more in attendance; the tiny handful of women delegates; the almost complete absence of delegates in their twenties and present-day players.'
Eugene McGee, writing on the rejection of special Congress proposals, *Irish Independent* (28 October 2002).

'I never ever want to hear anybody talking again about abuse of human rights in other countries. There is an abuse of human rights going on within the GAA, where everybody should have the right to represent themselves or be defended. Colin Lynch nominated two people to represent him to the Munster Council. They were locked outside the door.'

Ger Loughnane.

'The most striking thing about this body of people was their age. Grey and creaky clones in identikit suits, white shirts and sober ties, they looked like refugees from a Fianna Fáil ardfheis in the good old days. For these men, playing politics must be an awful lot better on the joints than playing sport.'

Miriam Lord, *Irish Independent*.

'This view is an attitude that is not only inaccurate and insupportable, but is also offensive to older people: the view that equates old with conservative, and young with progressive. This is a classic example of ageism.'

Michael Loftus, former GAA president (18 April 2001).

'Imagine a motion getting defeated that called for everyone being appointed to a position having the necessary qualifications. An Irish officer does not have to have any Irish, a coach does not have to be able to coach, presumably those in charge of finance don't need to be able to count. An extension of GAA logic to the real world would mean that a doctor would not have to study medicine and a solicitor would not need to know the law.'

Colm O'Rourke, *Sunday Independent* (17 November 2002).

'It is striking that after a summer of outstanding performance by amateur Gaelic football players which gave pleasure to record attendances, the attitude of officials to the GAA's greatest asset – its players – is rooted in an old command/ obedience model long discredited elsewhere.'

Letter to *The Irish Times* (3 October 2001).

'There is a level of politics in hurling. I don't think Henry Kissinger would have lasted a week on the Munster council.'

Ger Loughnane.

'I was interested to hear Peter Quinn, a most respected person in the GAA, admit that when he was president of the GAA 10 years ago he didn't have a clue what was going on in the association. I now realise I was sleepwalking through a serious GAA decline.'

Eugene McGee, writing on the rejection of special congress proposals, *Irish Independent* (28 October 2002).

'GAA officials still do not seem to realise the depth of hatred many players have for them. They need to learn fast and take decisive, conciliatory but fair action to sort out the money problem quickly. Judged by normal negotiation criteria it is not a particularly difficult problem to solve.'

Eugene McGee, *Irish Independent* (18 August 2003).

'One of the most noted unwritten rules in the GAA is that you don't argue with Frank Murphy. You will lose.'

Ian O'Riordan, *The Irish Times* (7 December 2002).

'We've got grounds which are state of the art and administration which is state of the ark.'

Ger Loughnane.

Overheard:
Hurlers on the Ditch

The greatest facility for the GAA fan is the capacity to remain anonymous. Overheard chance remarks have been part of GAA lore for decades. It has been known for the remarks to become embroidered and occasionally invented. The beauty is we never will know.

'I'm going to tape the Angelus over this.'
Meath fan, talking about his recording of the 2001 All-Ireland final.

'If they won't take you off, for f***'s sake walk off!'
Overheard in Armagh.

'There are two things in Ireland that would drive you to drink. GAA referees would drive you to drink, and the price of drink would drive you to drink.'
Sligo fan, on the 2002 Connacht final.

Fan: 'You have to talk to me, I paid good money. I paid ten quid in to see you play.'

Liam McHale: 'Do you think I saw any of your money?'
Keith Duggan, *The Irish Times* (10 May 2003).

'Jesus, if Lee Harvey Oswald had been from Mayo, JFK'd be alive and kicking.'
Overheard by Willie Joe Padden.

'He wouldn't see a foul in a henhouse.'
Fan, to a referee.

'Don't get yourself put off you bloody eeejit. Can't you do him in a friendly in Loughrea in a fortnight.'
Fan, quoted in Breandán Ó hEithir, *Over the Bar* (1984).

'Babs Keating resigned as coach because of illness and fatigue. The players were sick and tired of him.'
Offaly fan (1998).

'And as for you. You're not even good enough to play for this shower of useless no-hopers.'
Former Clare mentor, to one of his subs after a heavy defeat.

'When Joe Brolly is winning, he's objectionable. When he's blowing kisses, he's highly objectionable.'
Cavan fan.

'You might have at least taken your socks off!'
Overheard as a streaker was dragged off.

'Meath make football a colourful game – you get all black and blue.'

Cork fan (1988).

'We've won one All-Ireland in a row.'

Wexford fan (1996).

'Q: What's the difference between Paddy Cullen and a turnstile? A: A turnstile only lets in one at a time.'

Kerry fan, after Cullen conceded 5 goals in the 1978 All-Ireland final.

'Frank Cummins wasn't born, he was quarried.'

Fan, quoted in Brendan Fullam, *Hurling Giants* (1994).

'He'll regret this to his dying day, if he lives that long.'

Overheard, after Dublin's Charlie Redmond missed a penalty in the 1994 All-Ireland final.

'Meath players like to get their retaliation in first.'

Cork fan (1988).

'Bring Samuel home to Londonderry.'

Derry Protestant, talking as the team boarded bus for the final (1993).

'Most people know "langer" in Corkese isn't a German golfer with a putter as long as a three-prong pike. But did you know that the Kerry for "langer" is "ball of wax". As in when you shout at the linesman who semaphores his flag south instead

of north, "Go way ya ball of wax, ya." Or at least that's what it sounded like to me.'
Billy Keane (24 August 2002).

'That wasn't a kick in the backside, it was a pat on the back that slipped.'
Player, to referee.

'Referee, you are so crooked they will have to screw you into the grave.'
Fan, to a referee.

'Behind every Galway player there is another Galway player.'
Meath fan, on the 2001 All-Ireland final.

Player responding to a fan's comments: 'Oh, we have a comedian in the crowd.'
Fan: 'We don't need a comedian in the crowd, there are 15 you ye out there.'

'We're taking you off but we're not bothering to put on a sub. Just having you off will improve our situation.'
Manager, to a Derry player.

'In terms of the Richter Scale, this defeat was a Force 8 gale.'
Meath fan, talking after the 2001 All-Ireland final.

'Well yis carry spare hurls don't ya?'
Wexford player, after chucking a damaged boot towards the mentors expecting a replacement.

'Jaysus, he wouldn't hit Arnotts window wit a feckin brick.'
Dublin fan.

'The rules of Meath football are basically simple: if it moves, kick it; if it doesn't move, kick it until it does.'
Tyrone fan, talking after a controversial All-Ireland semi-final.

Announcer: 'Fógra… would patrons please note, that for safety issues, by order of the gardaí, that drinks… [pause]'
Fella in the crowd: 'Are on the house!' [Big cheer]

'Ye didn't win that many All-Irelands since they introduced helmets.'
Clare fan, responding to a Tipperary fan who was boasting about how many All-Irelands they had won.

'You'd think with all the fishermen in this county they'd be able to find a net to put behind the goals!'
Heard in Ballybofey, County Donegal, as the Donegal players emerged with footballs flying everywhere.

'I think Mickey Whelan believes tactics are a new kind of piles on your arse.'
Dublin fan.

'Come on Kildare. Do it for Shergar.'

"£127 a week? For that?'

'Jaysus, young Reilly, if you fell over twice you'd be at home.'

Overheard: Hurlers on the Ditch

'If it was a fish supper you'd have caught her.'

'Eddie it wasn't your fault, it the feckin eejits that picked ya.'

'Take that useless cluasán off, he's good for nothing. Take it easy on him. Sure the useless cluasán is my son!'

'I'm telling you now boy, you'll be in bed next week at 6 o'clock and that feckin Xbox is going in the bin as soon as I get home.
Father, at an under-10 match.

Pay for Play:
Cumann Largesse Gael

The GAA is the world's largest amateur sporting organisation. It managed to avoid acrimony over the pay-for-play issue through most of its history. But for how long more?

'Only Our Rivers Run For Free.'
Tom Humphries, envisaging a GPA song, *The Irish Times*.

'Money talks, often with seductive eloquence. But those who play Gaelic Football get no money for their efforts. For their years of dedication and struggle they may win glory. But they do not make money.'
Brendan Kennelly (1980).

'The man who works hard for money alone is not to be trusted.'
Colm O'Rourke, *Sunday Independent* (8 February 2004).

'GAA officials may frown at the notion of payment of managers but what better investment can a weak county make than to hire a knowledgeable football person with sound coaching skills to improve their county team and instill a bit of self-belief into the players?'

Eugene McGee, *Irish Independent* (20 September 2002).

'It got us a holiday in Australia.'

Páidí Ó Sé, on the 1985 Bendix controversy, one of the first sponsorship incidents.

'In football it is the winning combination that counts. The same applies to dosing calves.'

Mick O'Connell of Kerry, launching a brave new world of GAA players endorsing commercial products (1975).

'GAA executives should accept the validity of the Gaelic Players' Association and abandon the old bloody nonsense of burying their heads in the sand.'

Mick O'Dwyer, speaking on Radio Kerry (December 2000).

'The GAA aren't sharing their revenue with us; why should we have to share ours with them?'

Brian Corcoran, Cork player.

'It is to be hoped that Gaelic football will always remain as natural a game as it is today, and accordingly we trust that, while it will ever be developing on the scientific side, it will never become the possession of the professional player.'

Dick Fitzgerald, *How to Play Gaelic Football* (1914).

'In November I went to Detroit as part of the training pro-gramme for my job. Out there, far away from football, I wondered would I bother playing on my return. Why train as a professional, play in front of 30,000 paying people at Clones and get nothing for it? League of Ireland players are paid yet have much smaller crowds.'

Paul O'Dowd, Cavan goalkeeper, poet and writer.

'I don't think they'd admit it, but I think the Cork county board would think it [the players' strike in late 2002] was the best thing that happened.'

Alan Browne, Cork player.

'I get a good laugh from articles where some bloke protests his undying love for the county jersey and scorns profession-alism. I wonder how is his pub/shop doing or how many sales he might make on the road the next day. Some people gain benefit in kind from the GAA, most don't.'

Paul O'Dowd, the Cavan goalkeeper, poet and writer.

'Nearly fifty years since, Christy Ring was offered unimag-inable riches just to allow his name to be put over the door of a pub in New York. The tangler trying his arm was given a choice between disappearing in twenty seconds or taking a ducking in the Berwick Fountain.'

Kevin Cashman, *Sunday Independent.*

'The difficulty which Croke Park faced in dealing with the GPA lay in making sure that the issue of pay for play which would either sunder or kill the association never got off the ground. The GAA survives on voluntary commitment and that voluntary commitment continues so long as everyone appreciates that the people who put 20 or 30 hours a week into running a club or running a team are as highly valued as the players who put that time into training at inter-county level. The association survives in its unique and beautiful socialist splendour because deep down we know that despite his magnificence 79,000 people don't turn up in Croke Park to see D.J. Carey. They turn up to see their home place, they turn up as a function of history, geography, family and tradition. They turn up because it's their day out having worked and toiled and cared as much as D.J. over the years. And they expect that the money they spend will go to putting hurleys into the hands of the D.J.s of the future.'

Tom Humphries (2 December 2002).

'The GPA has been great for the morale of all the players. Even those who haven't joined yet will admit that they feel good about the way things are going, they see the good that has been done and the improvements that have come about.'

Anthony Rainbow, Kildare footballer.

'The GAA was preaching and practising sponsorships and endorsements and VIP boxes and premium seats and such-like ordinances springing from the three sovereign commandments of the new state religion: Thou shalt magnify and obey no other god than: 1. The Market; 2. Privatisation; 3. Globalisation.'

Kevin Cashman, *Sunday Independent*.

'It would always have been thrown back in our faces if things had not gone well. You just want to prove that what happened was justified and we always said that if all that stuff was looked after we'd be seriously competitive.'

Joe Deane, Cork hurler.

'Some of these GAA county players are behaving as if they want to get paid for enjoying themselves. The honour and glory of wearing the blood-red jersey was enough for Ring and the men of his generation and after all, they were the men who made Cork hurling what it is today. They were the men who won eight All-Irelands for Cork between 1941 and 1954 and they never complained about missing doctors or where they had to go to the toilet either.'

Eugene McGee, recounting a letter from the fictional Knocknavanna Gaels clubman Larry McGann (9 December 2002).

'They will scoff at the application from injured players for compensation. The men who risk life and limb are forgotten. The governing body has been captured by non-players and the players themselves seem to have no direct representation on it. It's time to wake up, take the bags from these gentlemen and show them the outside of the gates.'

James Kelleher, Cork hurler, letter of protest to *The Cork Sportsman* (11 August 1908).

'A lot of people seem to think I am getting thousands of pounds for my involvement with Kildare, but I get no more than the travelling expenses. I have set up a number of businesses in Kildare and that has helped, I suppose I have a stake in Kildare now. But I think that travelling expenses should certainly be paid to managers and I have no doubt that, in the not too distant future, they will have to pay managers also. Managers are being treated with contempt, but I think that the day is coming when that will change.'

Mick O'Dwyer, talking on Radio Kerry (December 2000).

'The solicitor told them not to attend any meeting without a shirt and tie although some of the lads didn't want that, says one source. In other words, if they were going to war they would do so in the proper attire.'

Cork player, during the 2002 strike.

'The whole heart of the organisation will be gone if the games go professional. I never want to see that. If you haven't the heart in the association, you have nothing.'

D.J. Carey.

'In my day, we had a few farmers, a few fishermen and a college boy to take the frees.'

Paddy Bawn Brosnan.

Philosophers All

The high rhetoric of the official GAA, and the deep passions of inter-club and inter-county rivalry, have meant that the GAA has accumulated a large body of proverbs, aphorisms and profound statements of its own. A thinker's game played by thinkers, surely.

'Cork bate and the hay saved.'
Johnny Leahy of Boherlahan, the Tipperary hurler, is said to have invented the phrase in the 1920s.

'Picasso said that to understand the Spanish you had to understand bullfighting and I think it was Paddy Kavanagh who said that you couldn't know the Irish without understanding the GAA.'
Kevin Myers, *The Irish Times*.

'In selecting the All Stars, one is spared the pain, there is no need to worry about where to put kick-outs, who will win breaks or who will cover for the flash player who gets all the publicity but who would not mark a man even if it meant saving his life, never mind his team. This then is a selection of very good players, not a team.'

Colm O'Rourke, *Sunday Independent* (August 2003).

'Preparing a team is like shaving. No matter how good a job you do, you still have to go and do it all over again the next day. Otherwise, you'll look sh**e.'

Pat Comer, sub goalkeeper on the 1998 Galway All-Ireland winning panel.

'Never be afraid of making enemies in hurling because deep down they're not your enemies at all.'

Ger Loughnane.

'An rud is annamh is iontach.'

Seán Óg Ó hAilpín of Cork.

'Every penny we put into soccer stays at the top. Most of what we spend on GAA trickles down.'

Weblog, 101 reasons why the GAA is better than soccer.

'Football talk is about eternal things: style, courage, determination, speed, cunning, complacency, waste, recklessness, the ability to work, intelligence, victory, defeat, renewal.'

Brendan Kennelly (1980).

'I think of myself as a socialist hurler. I'm not too bothered with scores as long as I win.'

Cormac Bonner, Tipprary hurler.

'The only scores to be settled are the ones that go between the posts.'
Charlie Redmond, Dublin footballer, on the Dublin–Meath rivalry.

'Play every match as if it was your last, but play well enough to ensure it isn't.'
Jack Lynch.

'Show me a good loser and I'll show you a loser.'
Jimmy Smyth, Clare hurler from the 1950s.

'The best hurlers aren't always on the ditch.'
Con Houlihan in a letter to *The Irish Times* on death of Jack Lynch (October 1999).

'I was there when Pat Fox scored that wonder goal with one hand in the replay against Cork. I remember well the roar that went up from the crowd and my young son said, "What was that?" "That," I said, "was the Munster championship."'
Ger Loughnane (September 1997).

'There is nothing even vaguely intellectual about a Munster hurling final, yet a proper enjoyment of the game pre-supposes a sophisticated appreciation of the finer things.'
David Hanly, Limerick-born wrier and broadcaster.

'In a street near Dublin's Croke Park, the Gaelic Athletic Association's stadium, two shops stand side by side. One sells hand-made dancing shoes, the other bespoke dentures. As a

summary of the physical and mental attributes required of those who play the game of Gaelic football, it is hard to beat.'
Harry Pearson (24 September 2001).

'We were dead in the water, we're still afloat.'
John O'Mahony, Galway manager.

'A Munster final is not a funeral. Although both can be a very sad affair.'
Ger Loughnane.

'I met very good full-forwards. I made them look bad.'
Jack Rochford (attrib.), Kilkenny hurler from 1900s and 1910s, quoted in Brendan Fullam, *Hurling Giants* (1994).

'In the dust of defeat as well as in the laurel of victory, there is glory to be found.'
J.J. Meagher, Tipperary county board chairman (1938).

'The All-Ireland Championship ruins your life.'
Liam McHale, Mayo footballer.

'All the great hurlers are emblematic of their era. The outlaw glint of Mick Mackey and John Doyle derived from a rough and ready rural way of life. Christy Ring's pioneer status and his eagerness to rush home for evening devotions on the day of a match marked him out as a typical puritan proof post-independence Catholic Ireland. The self-confident swagger of Eamonn Cregan, Babs Keating and Jimmy Barry Murphy had a lot to do with the new prosperity of post-

Lemass Ireland. Nicky English is, in many ways, the Celtic Tiger hurler, though he had retired from the game before the era was named.'

Eamonn Sweeney, *Munster Hurling Legends* (2002).

'Hurling – it's all a matter of inches, those between your ears.'

Kevin Armstrong, Antrim hurler and footballer from the 1940s.

'What constitutes a hurling county? Two All-Ireland and six provincial titles (Waterford)? Or 27 All-Ireland and 60 provincial titles (Kilkenny)? No All-Ireland and no provincial title (Carlow) but a lot of decent hurling people doing their best to promote the game?'

Martin Breheny, *Irish Independent* (3 June 2003).

'The GAA is chiefly a mindset and the abiding principle of that mindset is: All In Good Time.'

Keith Duggan, *The Irish Times* (10 April 2002).

'Hurling and sex are the only things you can enjoy without being good at it.'

Joe Deane, Cork hurler.

'It's memories of matches and fellas you played with that you'll bring to your grave.'

Donal Óg Cusack of Cork.

'When a truck hits a retaining wall, you don't gather up the fragments in a petri dish. Some things just happen. Like the wind sighs, the earth growls and games men play occasionally run against the grain of human science. Croke Park and

Thurles housed two epics that ended in draws and it's best not to feign knowledge of the genesis. Just breathe it in, folks.'

Vincent Hogan, *Irish Independent.*

'You can imagine Ireland just about without everything, but you can't imagine it without the GAA.'

Kevin Myers, *The Irish Times* (25 August 2004).

'As much won't do. You have to give more every year. That's the way it's gone.'

Pádraig Joyce, Galway footballer.

'The summer begins with the tribal longings but come September it's different. Croke Park on All-Ireland day is one of the last cultural experiences we share. Not having tickets for Croke Park on All-Ireland day is the other.'

Tom Humphries, *The Irish Times* (10 May 2003).

'Thurles encapsulated a conflict between the professional work ethic of teams and the stubborn informality with which the GAA treats them.'

Vincent Hogan, *Irish Independent.*

'Something about these thumping afternoons in Clones lets you know the championship is getting serious. Tight and intense, hard just to breathe – and that's only in the press box.'

Keith Duggan, *The Irish Times.*

'It's not just the richness of the sporting scene which makes the GAA central to Irish life, for it gives enormous texture beyond the pitch: the loyalties of parish, barony, county and province are shaped around the success of GAA teams. And Irish identity is almost contingent upon lesser, regional identities which slot neatly together to form part of the greater whole. Yes, hard to believe though it is, some men stand on tiptoe, their pulses quickening, when they hear the name Louth.'

Kevin Myers, *The Irish Times* (25 August 2004).

'How in the name of Christ are we to keep hurling going till next spring?'

John Maher, chairman of Kilmacud after a defeat.

'Why is the GAA shoving the premier match in our national calendar to a Saturday? I can't fathom the decision to play the replay on Saturday week, breaking completely with tradition for the sake of what is still, despite the hype, effectively a friendly game against the Australians?'

Mick O'Dwyer, criticising the decision to replay the 2000 All-Ireland final on a Saturday, *Irish Examiner*.

'There is a rhythm to these days and it is usually the rhythm of the cat and the mouse.'

Vincent Hogan, *Irish Independent.*

'As a chess game it was fascinating; as an Ulster final it somehow failed to fizzle.'

Cliona Foley, *Irish Independent.*

'This system will continue to keep hurling titles the preserve of the elite. To misquote scripture, those who have, will have more given to them, while those with little will lose that little.'

Letter to *The Irish Times* (6 September 1999).

'GAA goalposts cast nicer shadows on summer evenings.'

Weblog, 101 reasons why the GAA is better than soccer.

'The simple truth is that most GAA football matches are superior to most soccer and rugby matches as spectator sports; hence their vast crowds, while club rugby plays before what could pass for a bus queue, and even Leinster's early European matches draw the size of crowd you'd catch in the urinal at half-time in Newbridge.'

Kevin Myers, *The Irish Times* (25 August 2004).

'Perfection in sport is unattainable. Take a team sport like hurling then, with it's multiple demanding skills, multiply that factor by the 15 individuals involved on the field at any one time, add the input from the selectors, and the dream becomes even more impossible.'

Diarmuid O'Flynn, *Irish Examiner*.

'Television runs soccer. Schoolteachers run the GAA.'

Weblog, 101 reasons why the GAA is better than soccer.

'If putting on that county jersey doesn't motivate you, what will?'

Tony Scullion, Derry player.

'Keep you high balls low into the wind.'

Advice imparted to Kerry writer John B. Keane.

'We will win.'

Ger Loughnane, talking during a half-time interview with RTÉ during the 1995 All-Ireland final against Offaly.

'They were playing automatic football. When one Cross player won the ball another half-dozen began to set themselves up for participation in any one of several possible scenarios.'

Eugene McGee, *Irish Independent* (18 March 2000).

'Old soccer players get testimonials, old GAA players just slip down to junior. Dog rough it is too.'

Weblog, 101 reasons why the GAA is better than soccer.

'Yeah, because all you see are the two posts and the ball and the opponent standing in front of you with the hands in the air waving. It's just a matter of getting your mind clear, take your five or six paces back and two to the right and set it up and kick it over.'

Pádraig Joyce, Galway player.

'You can't play a defensive game of football or hurling.'

Weblog, 101 reasons why the GAA is better than soccer.

'Crossmaglen have some wonderful footballers but more importantly they have no bad ones.'

Tom Humphries, *The Irish Times* (18 March 1997).

'In Ulster the peasantry spent so long mired in neighbourly feuding that documentary teams rather than sports journalists used to cover the Championship there. Now they are standing on a hillock high enough to see the rest of the country.'

Tom Humphries, *The Irish Times* (10 May 2003).

'The GAA player who performs in front of 70,000 at the weekend will be teaching your kids on Monday or he'll be selling you meat or fixing your drains or representing you in court.'

Weblog, 101 reasons why the GAA is better than soccer.

'The GAA is about where you're from. Soccer is mainly about who you like.'

Weblog, 101 reasons why the GAA is better than soccer.

'The miracle of the GAA is that it works so well despite itself. Paranoia, self-doubt, trenchant conservatism, fear of outside sports and veneration of the past are all key parts of the GAA psyche. In order to love the GAA, you have to swallow these faults whole.'

Keith Duggan, *The Irish Times* (10 April 2002).

'Give me o'Lord a hurler's skill/With strength of arm and speed of limb/Unerring eye for the flying ball/And courage to match them whatever befall/May my aim be steady – my stroke be true/My actions manly – my misses few/And no matter what way the game may go/May I part in friendship with every foe.'

Seamus Redmond, 'A Hurler's Prayer'.

Refs, Roughs and Rules

Perhaps the most infamous incident in the GAA's entire history was the locking of a Wicklow referee in the boot of a car by irate supporters after a match. Undaunted, he was back whistling the following week. It sums up the spirit of the ref. The choicest phrases on the playing fields of Ireland each week are directed towards them, and still they carry on. They can even find time to indulge in a witticism or two themselves.

'Referees are like wives, you never know how they are going to turn out.'
John B. Keane.

'They shot the wrong Michael Collins.'
Ollie Murphy, to referee Michael Collins after Donegal beat Meath in the 2003 football championship.

'After the game is over is the worst time for referees. There is no police protection and it is quite true to add that the game may have been contested in a village where there never were police. His best bet here is to pick out the biggest man in the vicinity and to open a conversation with him. Those who are out for his blood can never be sure but 'tis his brother or maybe his uncle he is talking to.'

John B. Keane.

Referee: 'Who is refereeing this game, you or I?'

Pete Donohue of Cavan: 'Neither of us.'

'I didn't think they'd both get sent off. That was a bonus.'

Kevin Heffernan, the Dublin football manager, talking about the sending off of Robert Mulvaney and Pat Herbert during the 1988 Dublin hurling final.

'They managed to get a sub into the number eight jersey while his team-mates were arguing with the referee, so that their star player would avoid being sent off and appearing in the referee's report.'

Seán Óg Ó Ceallacháin, referee, *Tall Tales and Banter* (1998).

'He [the referee] must make the players feel he will tolerate no serious breaches of the rules. At the same time he must not err on the side of severity by keeping is whistle blowing like a foghorn at sea. He must be prepared to temper justice with mercy, and overlook, therefore, accidental infringements of the rules.'

Dick Fitzgerald, *How to Play Gaelic Football* (1914).

'It was the most cowardly thing I've ever done in my life. At half-time I said to the players, "Go out and die for your colours and for each other", and they very nearly did that. I was overcome when this late penalty happened. I believe in tough physical football, but I always said that the referee's position is sacrosanct, that they are beyond reproach. What I did yesterday I cannot understand.'

J.J. Barrett, Wexford manager and amateur pugilist (March 1999).

'Are you insured?'

Player, talking to Sean Óg Ó Ceallachain as he prepared to referee a game.

'This was supposed to be a game of football but I have to admit I was frightened for my life coming off the pitch.'

Seamus Prior, referee, after the Lavey–Skibbereen club football semi-final.

'A referee should be like a man. For the most part they are like old women.'

Billy Rackard, Wexford hurler from the 1950s.

'Lads, I won't put you off, you put yourselves off.'

Paddy Johnson, Kilkenny referee, speaking when he visited a team in the dressing rooms before a game, quoted in Brendan Fullam, *Legends of the Ash* (1997).

'No less than four languages were used on the field, Irish, English, German and bad.'

John Walsh, of Cratloe, in his referee's report of Meelick vs Ardnacrusha which was played during construction of the Shannon hydro-electrical scheme (1928).

'Once he ignores his enemies he is more or less ignored himself, but once he takes them seriously he is asking for trouble.'

John B. Keane, on referees.

'Why would you send us off? What will the crowd think? They came to see a county final, not a lawn tennis tournament.'

Mick Mackey, speaking to a referee, quoted in Brendan Fullam, *Hurling Giants* (1994).

'The referee turned down a request for a free and added, anyway from where you were, my mother would have scored.'

Seán Óg Ó Ceallacháin, referee, *Tall Tales and Banter* (1998).

'A referee who togs out in white is taken far more seriously than a referee who does not tog out at all. Like a singer who appears on stage wearing a dress suit, he has a headstart over those who treat the occasion lightly.'

John B. Keane.

'Hurry up and make a decision, ref. I have to go home to bale the hay!'

Player, during a club game in Derry as the ref dithered about whether to award a penalty.

'Following a long bout of booing he blew, and having blown could not remember why. The pitch was invaded but, completely in command, our friend raised his hand and announced that he had blown the whistle in order that two minutes might be observed. Nobody asked who was dead. It wouldn't do to exhibit such ignorance.'

John B. Keane.

'The referee should be as active on the field as most of the players. Consequently he should be a youngish man and physically fit to keep going from one end of the ground to the other. Our Irish temperament would appear to be more controllable in the hands of a referee who is familiar with members of the teams.'

Dick Fitzgerald, *How to Play Gaelic Football* (1914).

'Criticism is something you're going to get when you decide to put a whistle into your mouth. You've got to be able to accept that but above all you must rise above it the next day, no matter how bad a game you had or how good a game you had.'

Willie Barrett, hurling referee.

'The modern Gaelic game is far too fast for one field referee to manage.'

Peter Parry, Australian referee (1 October 2003).

'Referees, who it must be recalled are also human, are forced to watch and control actors, cheats, divers, liars and an ever-decreasing proportion of honourable men.'

Liam Griffin, Wexford hurling manager (April 2003).

'One thing I'd take from Aussie Rules: I'd let the defender stand where the foul occurred.'

John Bannon, football referee.

'The restraint in criticising in public our players for their mistakes is admirable. Why not the same for our referees?'

Connacht football final programme (2003).

'Hurling matches should be refereed by referees from hurling counties.'

Paddy Joe Ryan, Waterford county chairman.

'Referees in football and hurling are held in lower esteem than similar officials in any other sport. Some of this may be self-inflicted through inconsistent application of the rules but there is also a culture of disparagement which feeds the problem.'

Irish Times editorial (12 April 1999).

'The reluctance to accept that a referee got it wrong is based on the belief that if it happens too often, it will undermine officialdom and lead to a flood of appeals. It's a spurious theory and actually makes life harder on referees.'

Martin Breheny, *Irish Independent* (23 July 2003).

'If a player is making a genuine attempt to tackle but gets it slightly wrong I will award a free against him but won't tick or book him. I think that's a fair way of doing it but I will act if I think his foul was in any way deliberate.'

Pat McEnaney, referee, *Irish Independent*.

'The differences between the various categories of offence, e.g. rough play, dangerous play and striking or kicking, etc., are so vague as to be practically non-existent. The fact that set penalties are imposed for specific offences, e.g. rough play (caution/yellow card); dangerous play (one month suspension) and striking/kicking (three month suspension) makes a bad situation worse.'

Pat Daly, the GAA's head of games, 'The Need for Change' a note on disciplinary system (July 2003).

'I'd get rid of the most infuriating rule in the book, the Square Rule. That a forward has to stand there and refrain from playing the ball dropping in, while the keeper swans around like Rudolf Nureyev, is a mockery of the game.'

Gerald McCarthy, hurling manager.

'That referee was so biased they should appoint him for the football final as well.'

Meath hurling supporter, phoning *Sportscall*, the RTÉ programme, after the 2001 hurling final.

'As for abuse of players or referees. All it does is create an extra layer of noise.'

Donal O'Grady, Cork manager, talking at hurling symposium (15 November 2003).

'Unfortunately it is an insular game, confined to Ireland, and it does not have the international discipline controlling it as do soccer and rugby.'

Mick Doyle, *Sunday Independent* (15 August 1993).

'Referees are never consulted about rules. Congress pass them, we implement them.'

Fr Séamus Gardiner, official spokesman for the National Referees Committee.

Rough-Ups and Ruffians

In a contradiction, foul play is the source of high-minded disapproval throughout the GAA but in some quarters there is a fond and unspoken admiration for the rogue players who push the rules of the game to the limit and sometimes beyond.

'Pull first – ask questions later.'

Peter Coughlan, on the 1949 Cork vs Tipperary match, *Irish Press*.

'Several broken sticks, two broken heads, and two bruised fingers were part of the afternoon's play, for hurling, the Irish national game is the fastest and probably the most dangerous of sports. It is a combination of hockey, football, golf, baseball, battle and sudden death. It was a real Irish game. Except for one thing. There were no fights among the spectators and all true Irishmen know that you cannot have a good hurling match without a fight.'

Daily Mail, report on a match in Manor Park, London (1 October 1921).

'With deep sorrow the Gweedore Gallants announce the passing of the Dungloe Dodgers, on Sunday September 10th, 1961. Interment in O'Donnell Cemetery. May their hopes rest in pieces forever. Honorary coffin bearers – the Gallant Gallaghers, Jackie Coyle, Owenie McBride and Padraig McBride.'

Mock mortuary card printed before a Donegal championship match, quoted in Breandán Ó hEithir, *Over the Bar* (1984).

'The toughest match I ever heard off was the 1935 All-Ireland semi-final. After six minutes, the ball ricocheted off a post and went into the stand. The pulling continued relentlessly and it was 22 minutes before any of the players noticed the ball was missing.'

Michael Smith.

'There were the running feuds that appealed so much to my friends who tended the street corners and who longed for "the bit of slashing above in the Sportsfield" to bring a ray of sunshine into the tedium of a dull Sunday.'

Breandán Ó hEithir, *Over the Bar* (1984).

'That's the first time I've seen anybody limping off with a sore finger.'

Gene Morgan of Armagh, to his football team-mate Pat Campbell.

'Yesterday some friends entreated me in so pressing a manner to go to a hurling match that I (with shame must confess it) was not proof against their importunities, I accompanied them, but never could I imagine such cruelty could reign in the breast of man as I saw practiced there. The hurlers themselves often take away each other's lives by jostling, or pretending to strike the ball, when hovering in the air, and aiming at the same time with the greatest force at the temple of one of the antagonists. I have heard of several persons being killed on the spot and others never recover from their bruises received at this cursed exercise.'

Mr A. Ferrit, letter to the *Freeman's Journal* (13 August 1764).

'Who has not heard that hurling is a dangerous game? It is the most dangerous game ever played on the planet. The game was invented by the most sublimely energetic and warlike race that the world has ever known.'

Michael Cusack, *The Celtic Times* (26 February 1887).

'Immediately the pitch was the scene of a hundred battles.'

John D. Hickey, on the 1963 Leinster final between Offaly and Dublin, *Irish Independent*.

'The GAA is often an easy target for criticism when there are breakdowns in discipline. It is clear that such incidents on GAA fields receive far more attention and negative publicity than similar incidents in other sports. But instead of claiming to be victims we should strive to ensure that any breakdowns are limited and that our critics are denied the opportunity to attack and deride us.'

Seán McCague, GAA president, speaking to Congress (2001).

'I am sorry to say that the game was very rough and difficult to handle. T. O'Donnell (Kerry) was the first to retire injured and was replaced by T. O'Connor. Next came Jim Smith

(Cavan) bleeding from the mouth and nose. I am unable to say how he received these injuries. P. Devlin reported to me during the game that he had two teeth broken. Play was held up for five minutes owing to a spectator rushing the field and assaulting a Cavan player.'

Mr Hennessy, referee, in his report on 1937 All-Ireland football final replay between Kerry and Cavan.

'Ambulance men making their way through an angry throng, on their stretcher a semi-conscious man with his wounds still bleeding. No, readers, this is not a description of a riot in the North, it happened at the Colder–Ballyskenagh senior hurling encounter at the Barr venue last Sunday.'

Midland Tribune.

'On account of the drunkenness, disorder and consequent desecration of Sunday begotten by inter-parochial matches and tournaments held so often in Cavan in the last 12 months I feel it is my duty as a priest to withdraw altogether from the Gaelic Association. I hereby resign my figurehead position of president of the Slashers club.'

Fr Teevan CC, of Cavan in a letter to the Cavan convention (4 November 1889).

'The Wexford lads were a tidy, hardy active kind of fellow, the kind of lads to be found around a town.'

P.P. Sutton, sports correspondent, on the Wexford team of 1888.

'The average game of hurling today is good, but the average game of football is bad – the players commit too many professional fouls, and they can't blame it on the rules! Too many managers have a negative approach. They want to win at all costs, whereas in hurling, the players are urged to play the game to win.'

Micheál Ó Muircheartaigh, *Sunday Press* (8 August 1993).

'The myth grew up in the GAA particularly that when you went onto a playing field, you left the laws of the land behind you in the dressing room. As long as you were taking part in a match you had a licence to kick opponents, box them in the face, strike them with a hurley and generally behave like a savage. In the GAA there was a sort of general absolution extended to players who assaulted opponents by the great unwritten rule: "Whatever happens on the playing field should be left on the playing field."'

Eugene McGee (17 November 2003).

'The medics put on a big, stupid bandage which apart from the obvious staving the blood flow served two purposes: 1) it acted like a beacon to every Meath man in Croke Park. They might as well have stuck a target with the words "hit me" to my head; 2) the way the bandage was wrapped, it came down over my left eye, completely blocking my peripheral vision on that side.'

Ciaran McBride, Tyrone footballer, on the 1995 Meath–Tyrone semi-final.

'We're becoming too pansy-ish about our football. It's a game for men, for God's sake.'

Mick O'Dwyer, talking after the dismissal of Paul McDonald (a straight red) and Ian Fitzgerald (two yellows) during Laois' win over Offaly.

'I was barred from playing hurling for Newmarket on Fergus because the college directors said the game was too dangerous. Had he attended the 1967 Clare county final, he'd have concluded he was far too lenient in his judgement. All the players, bar three, waded in. When the dust cleared, those still fit to carry on were assembled in the middle of the field by the referee and given a stern talking-to. That wasn't the end of it, for a couple of gardaí and a superintendent marched out too. Irrespective of what action the referee took, the superintendent warned, he would arrest the next man who struck an opponent.'

Liam Griffin, Wexford hurling manager.

'There's a latent violence in Irish society, but what can we do about it?'

Jack Boothman, GAA president, after punch-up at 1996 All-Ireland final.

'Could I suggest that in future the GAA allocate a five-minute free-for-all before the television coverage of its games to dissipate the aggression, tension, etc?'

Letter to *The Irish Times* (October 1996).

'Five minutes of madness.'

GAA description of incidents at Parnell Park when the Dublin and Offaly teams engaged in a running battle during a Leinster under-21 championship match (1997).

'Eight or nine thousand people turned up to see blood and I ran around like a headless chicken trying to oblige. I hit Mark O'Reilly a couple of times off the ball, and tried to "do"

Martin O'Connell in a tackle. I remember him looking at me, almost laughing as if to say, you're four months late.'

Ciaran McBride of Tyrone, on the 1995 league match against Meath.

'Gaelic football is personal. It's not a kick around in the park early on a Sunday morning. It's not a run out for the boys.'

Liam Hayes, player and journalist, *The Title* (5 January 1997).

'He was lying on the ground there was a lad came out pouring water on his head telling him to stay down. That was annoying, but it was his first championship and if a fella tells him to stay down he'll stay down.'

Liam Dunne, Wexford hurler, on being sent off for the third championship in a row.

'We might have got on a goalpost and hung ourselves as try to get him off that night. Nobody up there [in Croke Park] was prepared to listen to us.'

Liam Dunne, reminiscing on his and Brian O'Meara's appeal against sending off in the 2002 All-Ireland semi-final.

'Legend has that it if on a hot day a group of players enter the baseball diamond at the corner of Gaelic Park and the sand rises, only the most battle hardened will be left standing when the dust settles.'

Paul O'Dowd, Cavan goalkeeper.

'About 10 minutes afterwards the ball came down my wing and Paddy beat me to it. All I could do was block him, he was hitting on the left side and I got a block in. I walked away, and next thing I woke up in the dressing room with Dr Stuart bringing me to with the bottle under my nose.'

Seán Óg Ó Ceallacháin of Eoghan Ruadh, talking about the day in Croke Park in 1951 when Paddy Donnelly of Vincent's hit him.

'The thumping, kicking and general punch-up which has become part of our TV enjoyment during the GAA All-Ireland championship is now as predictable as the unpredictability of the refereeing at these disgraceful free-for-alls.'

Letter to *The Irish Times* (7 August 1997).

'Why is it that violent play has now become virtually an integral part of Gaelic football at parish, county and inter-county level?'

Irish Times editorial (28 March 1997).

'If he was a horse he'd be glue by now.'

Benny Tierney, the Armagh goalkeeping coach, talking about Kieran McKinney's injuries.

'Gaelic football is what may be called a natural football game. There is no incentive in it towards rough play. One player can hamper or impede another in one way, and only one way, and that by means of the shoulder. Hence it is that severe tackling, rough handling and all forms of tripping are banned.'

Dick Fitzgerald, *How to Play Gaelic Football* (1914).

Rivalries

There are many more great rivalries than are listed here, but some seem to generate more discussion than others. Inter-county rivalry needs only a couple of meetings to become established – a close match or a disputed decision, and suddenly it acquires a broader cultural significance that impacts on every aspect of the county.

'Chuckle along to such classics as "Ye Pissed in the Powder!", "Ye're Only Feckin Stonethrowers!", "Ye've Only Two Seasons There, Pre-Season and Next Season!", "Ye'll Be Good If Ye Start Winning on Grass!", "Did Ye Let that Referee Outta the Boot Yet?" All lighthearted fun and guaranteed unoriginal.'

Tom Humphries, on inter-county insults, *The Irish Times*.

Clare–Tipperary (hurling)

'I'm not giving away any secrets like that to Tipp. If I had my way, I wouldn't even tell them the time of the throw-in.'

Ger Loughnane.

'We won two All-Irelands, and they were brilliant. But this was unique. People outside Clare would find it very difficult to understand just how much it mattered. This was the dream for every Clare person for decades – to beat Tipperary in a Munster final. Forget about All-Irelands. Had we won six All-Irelands and hadn't beaten Tipp in a Munster final, it wouldn't have been as good, but to win that day and go into the dressing room was sheer bliss.'

Ger Loughnane, *Raising the Banner* (2001).

'Loughnane had us driven demented. He said we'd never get the credit until we won another All-Ireland, that we'd never beaten Tipp in a Munster final, that he had dreamt of this all his life.'

Anthony Daly, on Clare-Tipp rivalry.

'Tipp–Clare isn't complex. It's simple as a street fight. Two teams on the edge of reason, hurling away until their chests caved in.'

Vincent Hogan, *Irish Independent.*

'Clare have come down to Cork on a mission to show people that we are no longer the whipping boys of Munster.'

Anthony Daly, Clare captain, 1997 Munster final speech.

'We wanted to go somewhere they don't know anything about hurling, and it was either Thailand or Tipperary.'

Ger Loughnane.

'That was the worst night of all. You could cut the tension with a knife and that shouldn't happen. You had young players there to play a game and all of a sudden there seemed to be a war on. I would say very little would have touched off a riot that night. If any serious incident had taken place on the field it would have set it off.'

Len Gaynor, former Tipperary manager, on Clare-Tipp rivalry at the 1999 Munster under-21 final.

'I know Nicky English did not start laughing at Clare lads, but they were laughing among themselves.'

Anthony Daly, Clare captain.

''Twas a few of the Tipperary players and fellas enjoying themselves, they had the match won. Those kind of things can be hurtful to the opposition. You must show respect.'

Len Gaynor of Tipp.

'Clare decided to approach the game as if they were playing Tipperary.'

Mike McNamara, Clare selector, on the 1998 Munster final between Clare and Waterford.

'Cork and Limerick have beaten us in more Munster finals in recent years than Tipp, yet no decent hurling person in those counties quibbled in the slightest.'

Ger Loughnane (September 2001).

'The day after the 1997 All-Ireland final, I was surrounded by six to eight reporters and the questions were fired at me. "What did I think of what was said in the build-up?" I held my cool and said I didn't want to get involved. I think it was the best way. It would only keep the thing stoked up. It was tough at times to keep a civil tongue but I'm glad I did. Very glad.'

Len Gaynor.

'We do not believe Len Gaynor's "I wonder what the Clare lads think now" quote attributed to him after the semi-final as we are most grateful for the great work he did here and believe he is a man of the highest integrity as are the vast majority of people in the great hurling county of Tipperary.'

Ger Loughnane (September 1997).

Cork–Kerry (football)

'A Kerryman and a Corkman were great pals but there was always that undercurrent of rivalry. When the Corkonian boasted that Cork County Hall was Ireland's tallest building the Kerryman contradicted him, "My innocent boy, isn't it well known that the climbers' hut on top of Carrauntuohill is the highest building in Ireland."'

Billy Keane (24 August 2002).

'I have to live next door to these Corkmen in Gneeveguila.'

Ambrose O'Donovan, Kerry captain, during his pre-match speech before 1984 Munster final.

'All the time I could see the skyline of New York getting clearer and clearer.'

Joe Keohane, Kerry full-back, remembering his two-minute argument with the referee in the 1947 Munster final after a penalty was awarded. He stood on the ball, pushing it deeper into the sticky Cork Athletic grounds mud. When Jim Ahearne took the kick it rolled harmlessly along the ground.

Cork–Kilkenny (hurling)

'Look back in ANGER – that is, in Admiration, Nostalgia, Gratitude, Elation and Reverence.'
Paddy Downey on Cork–Kilkenny rivalry, *The Irish Times* (12 September 2003).

'I don't want this quoted. I don't think our forwards are good enough.'
Kilkenny selector, talking before 1972 All-Ireland hurling final. Kilkenny won.

'We have no chance against this mighty Cork team.'
Paddy Grace, Kilkenny secretary, talking before the 1972 All-Ireland hurling final.

Cork–Meath (football)

'With Meath winning five Leinsters out of six at that time and Cork winning four Munster titles in succession, there had to be a few collisions – and some of it was not too polite.'
Colm O'Rourke, *Sunday Independent* (29 February 2004).

'In The Heat Of Battle – Nice Guys Finish Last.'
Sunday Tribune headline to a Colm O'Rourke piece on the 1988 All-Ireland final.

'The rivalry was intense, even bitter. There was little in the way of socialising with the enemy. Each side withdrew into their own. Meath players found that the affection and protection offered by their supporters grew in proportion to the vehemence of attacks from outside. It was easy to look on Cork as whingers if any of their players dared speak a word against us. They saw Meath as mean, cynical and calculating. Both sides fed off the stereotypes as it suited perfectly: next time round motivation wouldn't be a problem. Billy Morgan fed his passion, energy, even anger, into this. We were no different.'

Colm O'Rourke, on the 1988 All-Ireland final (29 February 2004).

'Meath gloried in intimidating Cork and resorting to fouling to retain their title.'

Dinny Allen, in response to Colm O'Rourke's comment.

Cork–Tipperary (hurling)

'You can't win derbies with donkeys.'

Babs Keating, talking before Tipp played Cork in 1990.

'Given the choice, Cork have played against the wind in the first half every time for more than 40 years. And their policy has been hugely successful: choice of ends has never been a factor in a Cork defeat in those decades. Tipp, on the other hand, tend to discuss and dither, and usually come down on the side of playing with the breeze if the toss is won. And many a Tipp man will tell you of many an occasion for bemoaning that choice.'

Kevin Cashman, *Sunday Independent* (7 June 1992).

Dublin–Kerry (football)

'Any All-Ireland you beat Kerry in is a double All-Ireland.'
Kevin Heffernan, Dublin manager.

'I love the Dubs… I love their irreverent wit and their amazing turn of phrase. The crowd on Hill 16 probably look on me as the common enemy when I bring a team to Croke Park to play against them, but I have always had a great relationship with Dublin supporters. I admire their passion for the game and the fervour they generate. There is no more intimidating experience for an opposing manager than to stand on the sideline and feel the ground reverberate with the chanting of "Come On Ye Boys in Blue". Beating Dublin in Croke Park is the benchmark of excellence.'
Mick O'Dwyer.

'A game between Dublin and Kerry represents the conflict between town and country, it gives a keener edge to normal sporting rivalry. Dublin has a lot of glamour and a big loyal following but I must say we get more satisfaction from beating them than any other team.'
Páidí Ó Sé, Kerry player (1985).

'Betcha those feckin culchies are holding up the traffic on purpose to stop us getting to the match.'
Kevin O'Shaughnessy, quoting a fictional Dub fan, *Irish Independent*.

'You could sense from the things people said that the Kerry–Dublin thing really did mean a lot. You could see the respect they had for the Dublin team. Paidí Ó Sé says he was never subsequently hit as hard as Dave Hickey hit him.'

Robbie Kelleher, Dublin footballer.

Dublin–Meath (football)

'The first time I brought the boys to a match they were chocked at the abuse being heaped on Seán. I kept trying to tell them it was the referee they were shouting at but they said, "Mammy, the referee isn't bald."'

Seán Boylan's wife.

Dublin–Offaly (football)

'In the '70s McGee and I would have spat at each other up and down sidelines, first when he was with UCD and I was with Vincent's and then when he was with Offaly and I was with Dublin. We would have disliked each other intensely. Now we can be civil to each other. Now we can have a chat and I think we're both surprised to find that we have a lot of views in common about the GAA. Back then, though, he was the enemy.'

Kevin Heffernan, on Eugene McGee.

'Dublin v Offaly, Jackeen v Culchie.'

Sunday Tribune headline, over Eugene McGee's column (1982).

Sky Blue:
Dublin's Seventies Social Revolution

One of the great GAA characteristics is how winning teams can transform every aspect of the community they come from, the popular and indeed social culture of its entire hinterland. When it happened in Ireland's capital, with its lopsided share of the population, the effect was magnified into a national event. The generation who witnessed the matches of the 1970s, in particular an acclaimed 1977 semi-final between Dublin and Kerry, have grown increasingly nostalgic for the euphoric innocence of that era.

'I have a distinct memory of walking down O'Connell Street sometime in the summer of 1974. It was a lovely sunny Saturday morning and I remember feeling there was a bit of a buzz. I said to myself it's great to be coming now. The economy was slumped. There was no soccer team going well. The rugby team were struggling. We were arriving. There was a space for us to make a difference.'

Kevin Heffernan.

'Our supporters put Dublin posters up beside their Manchester United ones. It was good for the game.'

Jimmy Keaveney.

'The 1974 semi-final was perhaps the greatest performance the fellas gave. I'd put it up there with the 1977 semi-final. Cork scored a goal at one stage with 16 men on the pitch. We just swept down and stuck it in the other end. In the final that year we were nervy and had to grind it out a bit, but in that game against Cork we played the way we wanted to play.'

Kevin Heffernan, on the 1974 semi-final against Cork.

'The Dublin players realised that everything Heffernan told them was coming true.'

Brian Mullins.

'I could see in his face what he was going to do.'

Paddy Cullen on Mike Sheehy's goal in the 1978 All-Ireland final.

'When Mike Sheehy is in town he will drop in. I tell him that I made him a star, he will say that he made me a millionaire.'

Paddy Cullen, interviewed by David Walsh for 'Goodbye to the Hill', *Magill* (1989).

'We watched the Kerry vs Roscommon match and reckoned that this was the difference between men and boys. We looked second division.'

Kevin Heffernan on the opening round of the 1974 Leinster championship. Dublin vs Wexford served as the curtain-raiser for Kerry vs Roscommon in the national league final.

'There were four fundamental points: the team had won nothing, it had done nothing, morale was at a low ebb and confidence just was not there. We wanted to create in the players a sense that they had an asset which nobody else had. We were going to make them the fittest team in the country.'

Kevin Heffernan, interviewed by David Walsh for 'Goodbye to the Hill', *Magill* (1989).

'Each year I associated the first smell of cut grass with the start of serious football.'

Gay O'Driscoll, interviewed by David Walsh for 'Goodbye to the Hill', *Magill* (1989).

'We went after certain guys. We had a style of play and demands on those who wanted to play it. Certainly character would have been an issue. We would have looked for guys who showed that, fellas who would make the commitment and be able to stand it. We wanted guys who could adapt. It wasn't everything though, the guys we ended up with were exceptional people.'

Kevin Heffernan.

'I played just once in 1973, I think. I was playing rugby the following year when Heffernan came looking for me and, to be honest, Kevin was pushing an open door. All I wanted to do was play with Dublin. If there was something serious happening with Dublin I wanted to play.'

Dave Hickey.

'We said everything that needed to be said and the lads were just getting up to leave when Gay O'Driscoll stood up and gave this passionate speech about how he was a sub the next day and if anyone in the room, anyone, felt like they weren't up to it, there was him and others waiting who would give their arm to be out there playing. He told them not to forget that.'

Kevin Heffernan.

'He stood there in the middle of the room, one hand in his pocket, just like F. Scott Fitzgerald and said, "Is that it?"'

Tony Hanahoe, on Dave Hickey's reaction when Heffernan announced his retirement in 1976.

'I think he left for the theatrical value of it. He gave no explanation. Just left us there. I think it was a betrayal.'

Dave Hickey, on Kevin Heffernan's resignation in 1976.

'I think the way Kevin walked away was bad and even worse was when he just came back after 1977. We had won a league and a championship under Tony Hanahoe and suddenly as if he'd hopped over the wire in Parnell Park he was back again and everyone moved over to accommodate him... I give Kevin credit for what he started. I just don't agree with the cult. He got us to All-Irelands but if you look back he has presided over more losing All-Ireland final teams than any other manager.'

Dave Hickey.

'In my view Heffernan was wrong about the media. Even if it was an evil, it still existed. But he saw it simply as an evil.'

Gay O'Driscoll, interviewed by David Walsh for 'Goodbye to the Hill', *Magill* (1989).

'In my view there were five footballers on the team: Paddy Cullen, Kevin Moran, Brian Mullins, Dave Hickey and Jimmy Keaveney. And of that five, Hickey never fully realised his potential. The rest of us were not footballers but we milked what we had to the fullest. The team was a great complement of talents.'

Robbie Kelleher, interviewed by David Walsh for 'Goodbye to the Hill', *Magill* (1989).

'What Kevin Heffernan did with the 1983 team was deserving of the highest praise. During the seventies he gave the orders and the lads got on with it. Cold and clinical. That was not going to work with the '83 team and Kevin changed his style. He cajoled them; he spoke with individuals outside of the group discussions and did many things completely different to the methods he used in the seventies. I would not have believed he had the capacity to change but I saw how he did.'

Tommy Drumm, interviewed by David Walsh for 'Goodbye to the Hill', *Magill* (1989).

'It got to a stage where I could look at a player running out on to the field for training and tell by the way he was carrying himself if there was something bothering him. They were men, mature, intelligent men. They had had choices. We can't go back and change any of it.'

Kevin Heffernan.

'I think Kevin had this thing about Kerry and rather than sit at home worrying about them he'd get the team down to Parnell Park so he could feel as if he was doing something.

The week before that final we did gruelling training sessions. We were over-trained. We did one night out in the rain for the benefit of the media. We came down on the Saturday and did another session. Then in the dressing room beforehand we did yoga for twenty minutes, something we'd never done before. We were supposed to be bouncing out onto the field and we hit the turf just glad to have survived the week.'

Dave Hickey, on 1975.

'I have worked with soccer managers who at the end of a team discussion would ask, "Has anybody anything to say?" Kevin never did that. He turned to somebody and said, "You. What do you think?" So in soccer I have rarely seen good team discussions, with Kevin we had them all the time.'

Kevin Moran, interviewed by David Walsh for 'Goodbye to the Hill', *Magill* (1989).

'There was an awful lot of tension in the banquet hall. Galway players not speaking to Dublin players and vice versa. Some Galway player had sung and a Dublin player was asked to reply. Joe McNally stood up and cut the air with a beautiful rendition of "The Fields of Athenry". In an instant all the tension disappeared.'

Tommy Drum, talking about aftermath of the 1983 All-Ireland final.

'You walked in the parade but only saw the legs in front of you and you never allowed your mind to stray. In the end if you won and there were a couple of seconds on the pitch when you savored it. That was all.'

Robbie Kelleher, Dublin footballer.

'I remember the colour of that day, the banners. It was personally uncomfortable, perhaps, to be at the centre of it but it was spectacular. You could feel that you were part of something new and unique.'

Kevin Heffernan, on 1974 All-Ireland final.

'If we had held on and won that match it would have been three in a row. That would have screwed them. I reckon Kerry would have done something stupid. Dropped half of them or got a new manager or whatever. Their confidence would have gone.'

Kevin Heffernan, on 1978.

'The success of the team brought the city alive. The crack on the Hill. In the pubs before and after the match, we could not be a part of that. Before the '74 final we were in the tunnel at Croke Park, on our way to the dressing room when a few of the lads ventured out to see what it was like. They saw the colour on the Hill 16 and said, "Hey, Jaysus, have a look at that."'

Robbie Kelleher, Dublin footballer.

'Study the equation: No Heffo = No Dubs = No Seventies = No GAA in the City = Slow Death for the GAA = This country being a Minor Colony of SkySportsSuperSunday-Land.'

Tom Humphries, on Kevin Heffernan (21 February 2004).

State of the Game:
Football

The most popular game in the country has a unique capacity for generating debate about the good old days, the bad old days, the bright new days, and the changes that are always necessary to make the game better. Making the game better is a little more complicated than it may seem – as each player, manager, referee, official and fan seems to be looking for different things from the grand old game.

'Football is a game for those not good enough to play hurling.'
Tony Wall, Tipperary hurler from the 1960s.

'In a certain sense Gaelic football of the present day is more scientific than any existing football game. In other forms of football, such is the constitution of rules governing them, there is very often too much of the element of luck. In the native game however, there is no such preponderance of luck, and this is to be accounted for by the fact that the rules provide the two kinds of score, the point as well as the goal. Everybody knows the tendency of outdoor games of the present day to reduce the individual player to the level of a mere automaton. In a manner, the individual in modern games is a disadvantage to his side, if his individuality asserts itself strongly, so strongly that he tends to be too much of an individualist and too little of the mere machine. How dry is the description one often gets of those great matches, in which perfect combination alone is the only thing commended. In them there is no hero, no great individual standing out from the whole field. If he did stand out, he would cease to be a machine, and is usefulness to the side would cease likewise. Such is the genius of the game itself, that while combination will always be prominent, the brilliant individual gets his opportunities times out of mind, with the result that, after the match is over, you will generally have a hero or two carried enthusiastically off the field on the shoulders of their admirers.'

Dick Fitzgerald, *How to Play Gaelic Football* (1914).

'It seems to a player who isn't winning that the GAA revolves around stronger counties. I always felt we are a little republic ourselves. We have to go and develop our own little support in our own county. We're not getting the publicity. We're not getting the honour that the stronger counties are getting. We'll have to enjoy ourselves in our own area.'

Jimmy Smyth of Clare, quoted in Colm Keane, *Hurling's Top Twenty* (2002).

'Was Larry Stanley roughed out of football? Did the same folk pull a similar stunt on Tommy Murphy? Were Down too scientific in the '60s? Was there no fitness before Kevin Heffernan pulled Jimmy Keaveney out of the bar in

St Vincent's? Which came first, the chicken or the egg, Mick O'Dwyer's vision of Kerry or the extraordinary players he had?'

Tom Humphries, *The Irish Times* (10 May 2003).

'Gaelic football is totally at peace with itself. It has, in truth, never felt more comfortable or confident about itself. The GAA sees itself as having the finest stadia in the country and the two greatest games in the country. Nobody's worried.'

Liam Hayes, footballer and journalist, *The Title* (5 January 1997).

'It was no accident that some of the best games of the 1950s and early 1960s were those in which the Dublin team was involved. Their attractive brand of combination football was almost totally constructive and they were never wont to adopt spoiling tactics to beat the other side. This was probably their undoing in not harvesting more championships but it was certainly conducive to open, continuous football.'

Mick O'Connell, Kerry footballer from the 1960s.

'There is no point in kicking the ball 50 yards to give the ball away because somebody suggested to play long football. You have got to retain possession, why not give it shorter and keep it?'

Mickey Harte, Tyrone manager, talking on *Off the Ball* on Newstalk 106.

'When I started my academic career in UCD in '92 I was amazed at how little recognition the GAA teams in the college got. I found it hard to believe that sports scholarships could be given to rugby players and inter-county GAA players weren't even recognised. Down the country, Gaelic football and hurling are the main sports but here it seemed that they were the poor relations to rugby and soccer. The rugby and soccer teams got the best training and playing fields that were nearest the dressing rooms in the sports centre. The GAA training pitch was an undersized muddy patch ten minutes walk away over the concrete concourse.'

Paul O'Dowd, Cavan goalkeeper.

'GAA fashion has moved on. So long mired in hell's millinery department, from where hats of finest crepe paper and cheapest fake fur dyed in the county colours were foisted on us; the GAA aficionado now stretches the county jersey over his gut or her bust. A small price to pay for dignity.'

Tom Humphries, *The Irish Times*.

'Bad and all as UCD was a friend studying in Trinity told me that that great institution was even more British in its sporting preferences. He complained that no game of GAA had ever taken place on the grounds of Trinity. Its playing fields were reserved for rugby and that other pathetic sport, cricket.'

Paul O'Dowd, Cavan goalkeeper.

'The lesser counties are like Oliver Twist, asking for more.'

Con Houlihan, *Sunday World* (21 September 2003).

'Sadly, the main contribution the Dublin footballers of the 1970s made – the hard-man approach – is still having an adverse effect on the game. Dublin were first to employ it – ask Mickey O'Sullivan – Meath took it a step further and

Cork and the northern counties developed their own hard men and won All-Irelands, just as Dublin did.'

Letter to *The Irish Times* (9 July 1999).

'In my long career I never remember [having] seen more determined games. Both counties gave football a fillip that marked, as it were, the starting point of the game as we know it today.'

Dick Fitzgerald, on the 1903 All-Ireland final between Kildare and Kerry.

'Some 40,000 people witnessed each of these strenuous tussles for supremacy and it has been said on all sides that never in the history of outdoor games in Ireland have people gone home so well pleased with what they saw.'

Dick Fitzgerald on the 1913 Croke Cup final between Kerry and Louth, writing in the introduction of *How to Play Gaelic Football* (1914).

'We feel bound to maintain stoutly that the fielding of the ball should ever be recognised as an essential and most attractive feature of our game, and the rules which secure this attribute of Gaelic football should be allowed to stand in the Gaelic code.'

Dick Fitzgerald, *How to Play Gaelic Football* (1914).

'Let it be written quickly: "P. Loughlin threw the ball into the Cavan net."'

P.D. Mehigan, sportswriter, on the 1928 All-Ireland final.

'Don Johnston, from Creeslough, featured in a player profile in the *Donegal Democrat* and, in response to a question on

how Gaelic football could be improved, he replied, "Make it 13-a-side." The Lord be praised! At long last, a player who actually deviated from such boringly repetitive lines as; improve refereeing standards/define the tackle/have a proper closed season.'
Martin Breheny, *Irish Independent*.

'The players nowadays have the same haircut our fathers wanted us to have back in the seventies.'
Billy Keane (24 August 2002).

'Kerry's brand catch and kick football is ten years out of date.'
Joe Lennon, *Sunday Press* (1968).

'Follow the centre line of the ball in catching and kicking; follow through a kick; never hesitate; clasp ball to the chest; pass only when necessary; cover opponent's kicks; hop the ball only to gain time; train on the weak foot.'
Dr Eamonn O'Sullivan, *Art and Science of Gaelic Football* (1958).

'It was absolutely crazy that so many sensible people started believing the nonsense that it was the northern way or no way. It irritated me because it made no sense whatsoever.'
Mike Sheehy of Kerry, quoted in Martin Breheny & Colm Keys, *Chosen Ones* (2004).

'I think Down did a lot of damage to Gaelic football. They broke the ball a lot and they played it very close and marked tightly. They weren't playing the ball that much but they played the man quite a lot. I suppose it paid dividends for

them. They fouled men in the centre of the field – and won All-Irelands with it. But it was not a good thing for the game.'
Mick O'Dwyer (1976).

'It is so long since I attended a football match I don't know how it is going to start.'
John Dillon, politician, who was invited to throw in the ball at the start of the 1913 All-Ireland final.

'Most of those disgusting rules which made the training of twenty years ago such an awful bugbear have now been discarded and a more rational system is even now in vogue.'
Freeman's Journal, commenting on the Civil Service atheltics club sports (27 May 1872).

'It is forgotten that not all war-time big games were graceful affairs – indeed the football All-Ireland of 1943 could charitably be described as a thundering disgrace.'
Con Houlihan, *The Back Page* (1999).

'It is not so very long ago, since the very knowledgeable people were shaking their heads and dishevelling their hair over what they pronounced the corpse of Kerry football. Kerry, they said, had paid the penalty for being too rigid and tradition bound. The game had passed them out. Failure to adapt to new ideas and new methods had found Kerry lagging behind. And while Down and Galway and others were dividing the spoils between them, the funeral of Kerry football was being well attended by those who could hardly catch and only kicked when no alternative appeared.'
Notes in the 1970 All-Ireland final programme.

'I think it's a bit outdated to suggest that everyone should remain in their position, a sort of blanket formation, which is what people mean by the catch and kick game, which is outdated in the modern flexible game. Who in their right mind would stand and let someone catch the ball?'

Joe Lennon, *Fitness for Gaelic Football* (1968).

'We have always made a clear distinction between the man who is fleet of foot and the man, not necessarily over fast, who is ready to do what is to be done.'

Dick Fitzgerald, *How to Play Gaelic Football* (1914).

'Undistinguished, unexciting, cheerless and insipid.'

John D. Hickey, on the Kerry vs Roscommon 1962 All-Ireland football final, the worst in living memory.

'Don King has a theory that the surest way to success is to whip up as much confusion as possible, on the basis that opportunities are certain to emerge amid the ensuing mayhem. Let King loose on some of the crazy rules of the club championships and he would happily change his familiar catch phrase, "only in America" to "only in the GAA".'

Martin Breheny, *Irish Independent.*

'There are three things which tend to make the playing of football, and in a sense the playing of every outdoor game specially difficult, and these are the sun, the wind and the rain.'

Dick Fitzgerald, *How to Play Gaelic Football* (1914).

'There is a need to think about the game, not in the way we have been thinking for the past sixty years but in a way that is in keeping with the tenor of mid-twentieth-century life. It is only by keeping the game up with the progress of social, educational and scientific reform that we can hope to make it acceptable to the age in which we live.'

Joe Lennon, Down player and theorist (1963).

'The Ulster Championship, of which each installment was once known as The Pullers and Draggers' Big Day Out has opened up and allowed itself to breathe.'

Tom Humphries, *The Irish Times* (10 May 2003).

'Gaelic football is like rugby league, rugby union and soccer in that it's three-quarter pace stuff.'

Donal O'Grady, Cork manager, talking at a hurling symposium (15 November 2003).

'We only ask for a chance that players who are not wanted by Dublin teams to assist counties where they have trained.'

P. Fay of Cavan, proposing the 1925 declaration rule.

'The game is called football, not handball. The guiding philosophy should be that the main means for transferring the ball from one end of the field to the other is by kicking it. In the past 25 years this fundamental principle of the game has become debased because of the short passing culture adopted by so many managers and coaches. Explain to players that you cannot run with the ball or handpass the ball over a space of 40 or 50 yards as fast as the ball will travel over the same distance if it is kicked.'

Eugene McGee, *Irish Independent.*

State of the Game:
Hurling

Everybody agrees hurling is beautiful to watch and play, the wonder is that anyone agrees on anything else that relates to the game.

'Hurling is the *Riverdance* of sport.'

Liam Griffin, Wexford hurling manager.

'We started a new thing, standing all square and pucking the ball out of the sky at the last second. It's all the ploy now. They are all putting their hand up. That was new. I think we invented that. Every time we got hold of it, it went way up-field. We wouldn't be noted for ground hurling or for good overhead striking.'

Billy Rackard, Wexford hurler from the 1950s, quoted in Colm Keane, *Hurling's Top Twenty* (2002).

'Here is one dangerous preconception, the notion that, in a traditional county, greatness is easily acquired. That marquee names like D.J. Carey and Henry Shefflin just take their gifts blithely from the womb and simply free wheel. In essence, the idea that a Kilkenny hurler can amble to All-Ireland glory.'

Brian Cody, talking at a hurling symposium (15 November 2003).

'When we were kids, getting on a bus with a hurley meant hearing none-too-subtle remarks about boggers and rednecks and gahmen. The games have a different cachet now, for some reason we can't understand but have to welcome.'

Tom Humphries (12 May 2003).

'Picking, lifting and handling are widespread faults, and after much consideration I have come to the conclusion that handling through the field should be made illegal. Ar an dtalamh (on the ground) was the mantra of the old teachers.'

P.D. Mehigan, *The Irish Times* (January 1930).

'With hurling becoming faster, players can't afford the risk of slowing their reactions. Hurling is a game of such quick reaction, that even watching a game of football can affect you.'

Justin McCarthy.

'I always felt – and I played the game all my life – that there was a certain dignity about hurling whether you win or lose. I always had great respect for my opponents.'

Len Gaynor.

'In the old days the emphasis was on backs stopping forwards from playing. Now it's more positive. Full-back is a prime example. Nowadays he has to be one of the best hurlers. The lighter ball is a huge factor.'

Gerald McCarthy, Cork hurler and inter-county manager.

'Never put your hand up when you can put your hurley up.'

Eamonn Cregan, repeating the advice he got from his father, quoted in Brendan Fullam, *Legends of the Ash* (1997).

'It's part of our culture. It's part of who we are as people. I think it's a tragedy that so many Irish people don't know anything about hurling.'

Liam Griffin, talking on *The Dunphy Show* (September 2003).

'Lines scribbled on a map by some Elizabethan clerk in the 16th century have determined, for instance, whether a hurler lives in the hurling graceland of Kilkenny or the neighbouring wasteland of Carlow.'

Tom Humphries, *The Irish Times* (10 August 2002).

'If you think that by intellectualising coaching you can make kids better, you're wrong... Most top hurlers honed their skills against a wall.'

Liam Griffin, Wexford hurling manager, talking at a hurling symposium (15 November 2003).

'We put a lot of time into players tussling, tackling for the ball. Getting their bodies in. It tears the guts out of them. They hate doing it. But they begin to like it, the closer it comes to the big games.'

Brian Cody, talking at a hurling symposium (15 November 2003).

'You couldn't even begin to imagine the time people like D.J. and Henry and J.J. Delaney spend trying to perfect their skills.'

Brian Cody, talking at a hurling symposium (15 November 2003).

'They cannot hit a decent ball on the sod, cannot double with direction on ground or overhead, cannot strike a flying drop with any reasonable degree of accuracy. Perhaps it is for want of sound tutor. Perhaps it is that the age of speed at all costs, allied to the current craze for the spectacular, has left its mark on our ancient game.'

P.D. Mehigan, sportswriter, *An Ráitheacháin* (June 1936).

'One thing I find hard to understand is why midfielders and half-backs, and often wing-forwards too, don't use the lift and strike more. I mean, a fellow controls the ball, then he handles it, now he has to throw it up again. He's given the opponent a better chance to get to him and spoil him. And the fellows up front are getting the ball that fraction later.'

Gerald McCarthy, Cork hurler and inter-county manager.

'You need split-second control, instant first touch. And you don't get those out of a book. You get them by practising.'

Brian Cody, talking at a hurling symposium (15 November 2003).

'It is said to be the original form of hockey, some people have described it as hockey without rules. Hurleys meet in the air with a wild crackling of wood, one of them is broken into two pieces, and small boys rush onto the field in a struggle to retrieve a broken blade as a memento. The casualties to sticks certainly went into the double figures. The casualties to players were less numerous, but the ambulance men must have been on the field eight times. It is certainly a swift and beautiful game, calling in to play all the skills of eye and hand and foot. Even when a game is one-sided, an invincible player can keep it exciting to the end.'

Robert Lynd, on the 1934 All-Ireland hurling final.

'I remember one day in New Ross when Dick Cantwell in goal pucked out, it was doubled on in midair by Lory Meagher and Willie Wedger Brennan doubled again to score a point without the ball hitting the ground.'

Martin White, Kilkenny hurler from the 1930s, quoted in Brendan Fullam, *Hurling Giants* (1994).

'Porridge, brown bread, raw eggs, and a wee drop form the craythur.'

Willie Barron, Waterford hurler from the 1940s, talking about the secret of becoming a great hurler and subsequent longevity, quoted in Brendan Fullam, *Hurling Giants* (1994).

'When you make a mistake, don't let the whole place know you are after making a mistake. We all make mistakes, all the players do. But keep your mistakes to yourself.'

John Keane, Waterford's inspirational hurler of the 1940s and 1950s, quoted in Colm Keane, *Hurling's Top Twenty* (2002).

'In Kilkenny they very notably think long and hard about the game of hurling – sometimes to the extent of outsmarting themselves. In Cork we think long and hard, too, except that much of what we think is complacency or cliché; in Tipp it is self-delusion; in Clare paranoia; in Wexford nostalgia; and in Limerick grudgery.'

Kevin Cashman, *Sunday Independent* (2003).

'Scribblers are bankrupt of phrases. Our vocabulary is exhausted, we must invent a new language to describe modern hurling, 1940 was as like 1939 as two stacks of sound grain in adjoining harvest fields.'

Cork Weekly Echo report on the 1940 Munster final.

'Hurling's reticence goes to something more fundamental. There is a selfishness among the upper classes, a contentment with the status quo. The odd missionary, a Dinny Cahill or a Michael O'Grady, goes forth to the counties of hurling's primitivism and tries to teach the natives but collectively hurling doesn't do enough for its toiling classes.'

Tom Humphries, *The Irish Times* (17 May 2003).

'God be the hurling of our time. Doubling on the balls from the sky. Nowadays they're putting their hands up to catch it, the opponent who pulls is blown for dangerous play.'

Jack Lynch, talking to Waterford's Mick Hayes in 1948, quoted in Brendan Fullam *Legends of the Ash* (1997).

'The more stitches required after a game in the Cork dressing room, the more probable they had won.'

Con Murphy, the Cork team doctor.

'Nobody has ever scored goals on a consistent level like DJ. Outstanding goals. So, naturally enough, people focus on his first touch, his striking on the run. But, having worked closely with him for the last few years, to me what separates him from the rest is actually his tackling ability. His hooking and blocking – people don't concentrate on those skills enough. But in Kilkenny we do.'

Brian Cody, talking at a hurling symposium (15 November 2003).

'Players with the natural talent to excel in hurling and football are being forced to make a choice and I, for one, regret that.'

Brian Murphy of Cork.

'If counties like Antrim or Westmeath are to beat Tipperary of Kilkenny, a hurling atmosphere has to be nurtured and cultivated in these places. I am more than ever convinced that, given a hurling environment, the most important single factor in the development of hurling skill is to ensure that from the earliest possible age the potential hurler has got the proper grip of his hurley.'

Tony Wall, Tipperary hurler from the 1960s (1975).

'I meet so many bullshitters in the GAA, who are going to do so much. They talk all day about hurling, never shut their mouths. And, yet, they're never seen in a field.'

Liam Griffin, Wexford hurling manager, talking at a hurling symposium (15 November 2003).

'We never took photographs before a match. Bad luck.'

Tom McInerney, quoted in Brendan Fullam, *Legends of the Ash* (1997).

'There will never be games, believe me, to equal those two games at Thurles in 1940.'

Mick Mackey, talking to Raymond Smith about the Cork vs Limerick draw and replay in the 1940 Munster hurling championship (1974).

'The most skilful player in the world won't necessarily win a game for you... The guy who's gonna do the business for you is the one who takes responsibility. He's not going to hide, not going to just mind his own position. Winning or losing games comes down to people being prepared to be unselfish.'

Nicholas English, talking at a hurling symposium (15 November 2003).

'Tommy Maher masterminded the 1957 All-Ireland win, which put an end to a worrying period of Wexford hegemony in Leinster and beyond. Kilkenny responded to Wexford's physical presence scientifically, playing low diagonal balls, skipping out first to the ball and delivering it quick off both sides.'

Diarmuid Healy, Offaly hurling manager from the 1980s.

'No other school, not even St Flannan's, has the influence on the affairs of the county team Kieran's has.'

Tom Humphries, on St Kieran's relationship with Kilkenny hurling, *The Irish Times*.

'In 1975 in Kilkenny I remember we won the senior, under-21 and minor All-Ireland titles and all the talk was would anybody ever beat Kilkenny. I spoke at a dinner that winter and I said when empires are at their greatest that's when they are most likely to crumble. We didn't win a thing the following year.'

Diarmuid Healy, Offaly hurling manager from the 1980s.

'This concept of a "born hurler" is a total myth but sometimes myths can be more powerful than truths.'

Con Houlihan, *Sunday World* (June 2003).

'If you happen to be born in the wrong part of the country you can't play. Hurling is neglected when children are denied the right to play it. We're lacking the will.'

Liam Griffin, Wexford hurling manager from the 1990s.

'It's not so long ago since there were six or seven counties capable of winning the All-Ireland but, for the present, that's not the case.'

Jimmy Barry Murphy, Cork hurler from the 1970s and hurling manager in the 1990s.

''Tis all in the wrist. A flick of the wrist. That's all that's needed.'

John Keane, Waterford's inspirational hurler of the 1940s and 1950s, quoted in Colm Keane, *Hurling's Top Twenty* (2002).

They Also Serve

Every team, every club, every county and venue has a small army of people put in place to deliver the mass consumer product that is Gaelic games. They are universally enthusiastic. No wonder things sometimes go awry.

'If they win, I'm not bringing them home.'
John Shelley, a Tipperary man given the job of driving a coach load of Clare fans to Dublin for the 1997 All-Ireland final.

'Urgent message… would the Westmeath bus driver please return to the bus.'
Announcer, at the 2003 league final.

'Some of ye may know the announcer in Tullamore a few years ago (not sure if he's there now) but at the county final a few years ago just after the band played the national song and all that they were heading off the pitch. So the tension is beginning to rise with the crowd getting a bit vocal and the

announcer comes on the speaker, all ready you get into action, and says, "For God's sake, will the band ever get off the pitch the game's about to start."'
Weblog, GAA anecdotes.

'Would patrons who have parked their cars in the car park not move them until the rest of the crowd have passed out.'
Announcer, at Armagh league game in Crossmaglen.

'So much of sports psychology is common sense but not common practice.'
Liam Hackett, sports psychologist with several GAA counties in 1980s and 1990s.

'The gate money has just been stolen.'
Announcer, at Casement Park (1984).

'Patrons who want to go to the toilet should use the passage under the stand.'
Announcement, at half-time in the 2003 Meath vs Westmeath game at Portlaoise.

'The biggest problem is the misidentification of sports psychologists as faith healers or spoon benders, like an Eileen Drewery or a Uri Geller.'
Dr Aidan Moran, UCD based sports psychologist.

'Number 23 Eamon Taaffe replaces... who's he replacing... oh yeah... Barry Murphy.'
Announcer, at a Tipp–Clare league game in Ennis.

'The girls at the Armagh shop would be happy if patrons could relieve them of their goods.'

Announcer, at an Armagh league game in Crossmaglen.

'I asked them for one reason Wexford would beat Offaly on Sunday. Liam Griffin and the other members of the management team were sitting together and I prayed that none of them would crack and say something. I caught Griffin's eye and sensed that he grasped the importance of biting his tongue. I thought, Oh Jaysus, I've blown it. They're going to be deflated now. It was five minutes before anyone spoke. One word borrowed another and before the session ended every member of the panel had made a contribution. We had 30 reasons Wexford would beat Offaly. If you were to paint that room a colour... it started off insipid green. It was kind of, "Aw, I don't know – I'm feeling a bit sick." And it turned into a vivid, vibrant red to the point where Liam Dunne went home and said to his mother, "We decided today that we're going to beat Offaly."'

Niamh Fitzpatrick, the Wexford sports psychologist.

'No one knows if mascots actually enjoy Gaelic football as they never applaud or praise their team. Rather for 60 minutes, the mascot, foaming and frothing at the mouth, curses the opposition, the referee, his own team, etc. Most mascots cannot drive, yet there is a goodly soul in every club who persists in bringing this person to away matches.'

Weblog, on mascots.

Through the Field

The positions on the GAA field seem to attract different types of personalities. Goalkeeping, the position of Albert Camus, Pope John Paul II and Patrick Kavanagh, has a philosophy of its own that non-goalkeepers can never quite understand. But so it is with backs, midfielders and forwards as well.

Goalkeepers

'The goalkeeper should fight always against the temptation to grow careless and dispirited when a goal is registered against him. Whether the score has come as a result of a mistake on is own part or not, he should be so minded as to play until the last whistle with the utmost confidence and cheerfulness. He must bear in mind at all times that everybody who has an intelligent knowledge of the game will appreciate the responsibility of the position he occupies in goal and will be prepared to make every allowance for the difficulties which, if necessary, it entails.'

Dick Fitzgerald, *How to Play Gaelic Football* (1914).

'Goalie – must have "great goalmouth presence"... which is secret code for being fat enough to have his own gravitational pull. The last time he got his knees dirty diving was at a céilí in 1965 when his version of the Hucklebuck went out of control.'

Weblog, GAA positions.

'Keep close to the goal today, I didn't bring any oxygen.'

Billy Morgan, Cork goalkeeper, to his full-back.

'The Dublin goalkeeper was playing in the centre of the field where his presence was often not needed.'

Freeman's Journal, commenting on the 1897 All-Ireland football final.

Backs

'Know your own position. Play it. Be in command.'

Justin McCarthy, Cork hurler, quoting Fr Roch, an influential coach from his youth, in Brendan Fullam, *Legends of the Ash* (1997).

'Fellows looked after their own corner, their own part of the field. That was traditional. That was the way it was done.'

Dick Stokes, Limerick hurler from the 1930s, quoted in Colm Keane, *Hurling's Top Twenty* (2002).

'We cannot help saying that there is great room for improvement to nearly all our full-backs up and down the country in the manner of kicking running balls. True it is that there is a tendency on the part of the greatest exponents of the game to pick up the ball with the foot, transfer to the hands, and get in a long punt. If that excellent feat can be executed with great rapidity, we must admit that it is all that can be desired. But unfortunately there are occasions when a back has not time to stop or stoop to handle the ball. The ball must then be kicked as it runs, or the situation is lost.'

Dick Fitzgerald, *How to Play Gaelic Football* (1914).

'A real hateful, sticky hoor. A lad that would just be up your hole the whole time.'

Ollie Murphy of Meath, waxing lyrical on the type of corner-back he dreads.

'A No 3 who fails to assert himself is on his way to being No 23.'

Mick Lyons, Meath full-back from the 1980s.

'Wicklowmen I knew were experts on atin' cocky corner-forwards without salt.'

Liam Griffin, Wexford hurling manager from the 1990s (April 2003).

'Corner-back can be quite a restrictive position, you don't get much of a chance to do much hurling.'

Frank Lohan, Clare hurler from the 1990s.

'The first duty of defenders (that is all players on the team, who have not got the ball; try to get this point across clearly, all players, even corner-forwards become defenders when the opponents have the ball) is to minimise the scoring chances of the opposition. Regardless of which opponent has the ball, all defenders in the vicinity of the ball should help in recovery.'

Joe Lennon, *Fitness for Gaelic Football* (1968).

'Playing extra defenders in such a blatant manner is frowned upon in the GAA on the basis that it concedes the psychological advantage to your opponents, an argument which has little substance in reality.'

Eugene McGee, *Irish Independent*.

'A very little reflection will convince one that the defence must be beaten before any score can be registered against them, and the defence is usually beaten by being drawn, as footballers say, or deceived by some ruse or other.'

Dick Fitzgerald, *How to Play Gaelic Football* (1914).

Midfielders

'Midfielder – chronic alcoholic who last scored a point in the late 70s and yet reckons he is justified in having a go for a point from anywhere inside the opposition's half.'

Weblog, Gaelic football positions.

'We do not count on the two midfield men for regular and defined combination, for they are supposed to have a roving commission.'

Dick Fitzgerald, *How to Play Gaelic Football* (1914).

'I'd see the trajectory of every kick and knew when to go for it. Two handed for the reasonable ones, pulling down the high ones one handed. Go up like a diver feet together. Come down like a hurdler on one foot and kicking with the other. The momentum gave me length and I'd have a map in my mind where the forwards were.'

Pat 'Airplane' O'Shea, Kerry footballer from the 1910s.

Forwards

'Centre-forward – third of the set of brothers that includes the full-back and midfielder. Is the target of all the brothers' clearances – all of them.'

Weblog, Gaelic football positions.

'It would appear desirable to look for good height and a fair amount of weight in the centre one of the three scorers. If notwithstanding the centre scorer be rather on the light side, he must have other compensating qualities. The Irish saying applies to this case, the man who is not strong needs to be cunning.'

Dick Fitzgerald, *How to Play Gaelic Football* (1914).

'Full-forward – hasn't scored since the end of the war but is captain of the team and an all-out nutcase. The line commonly quoted to excuse his complete inability to find the target is he's a good man to bust up the play.'

Weblog, Gaelic football positions.

'Left corner-forward – the village thug, who invariably sports an earring and a seriously dodgy haircut. Will be involved with the referee within five minutes of the throw in. Plays the foreign game with the town five miles down the road and is hence viewed with suspicion by all and sundry. Has had a

running battle with the ageing club secretary who secretly fears for the virtue of his youngest daughter.'
Weblog, Gaelic football positions.

'Occasions will occur when the centre-forward, after passing the ball on to either scorer, may expect the latter to re-pass to himself. All this manoeuvring is feasible enough between competent men who know one another's play.'
Dick Fitzgerald, *How to Play Gaelic Football* (1914).

'Wing-forwards are playing like backs and teams field four forwards at most.'
John O'Keeffe (27 September 2003).

Captain's Calling

'In forty minutes I am going across for that cup and I want you all behind me. Here is my speech.'
Eamonn Grimes, Limerick hurling captain, giving his half-time speech for the 1973 All-Ireland final, as he put a note in his stocking.

'In the 1946 All-Ireland, Jimmy Murray went off injured with about 10 minutes to go. Those attending his facial injury were careful to wash away the all the blood so that he would look well and presentable when he went up to receive the cup.'
Gerry O'Malley, Roscommon footballer from the 1960s, quoted in Brendan Fullam, *Hurling Giants* (1994).

'I was the non-playing captain.'

Dinny Allen, Cork footballer from the 1980s, speaking after captaining Cork to win the All-Ireland in 1989.

'The finest players are often sacrificed if they be placed under an incapable leader.'

Dick Fitzgerald, *How to Play Gaelic Football* (1914).

Tools of the Trade

A good workman never blames his tools – something that would never happen in Gaelic games, surely?

'A Tipperary man named Blake told me before the 1956 All-Ireland that I shouldn't put on my boots until I was ready to go out. I asked him why and he said – don't you know what when you saddle a horse he begins to prance. Ever after I didn't put on my boots till all were ready to go out.'
Jim English, quoted in Brendan Fullam, *Hurling Giants* (1994).

'I know Jack [Fitzgerald] had donned an overcoat and when the ball happened to come his way he had first to take off his overcoat.'
Patrick Ramsbottom (Thigeen Roe), *Leinster Leader* (March 1907).

'Had the new rules been in place during the nineties, and those two extra poles been erected either side of the goals, Kildare would definitely have won the All-Ireland on the strength of their ability to kick the ball narrowly wide with great regularity. Mayo too might have got their grubby hands on the Sam Maguire, but I'm not so sure about them because no matter how vast the scoring target is, they'd probably still manage to miss it.'

Kevin O'Shaughnessy, *Irish Independent* (18 October 1999).

'A Christian brother at school used to ask us who won the All-Ireland minor title in 1948. We would all say, "Waterford." "And who should have won the All-Ireland title in 1947?" "Waterford," we would answer. "And why didn't they win it?" "Because they all hadn't cogs on their boots."'

Austin Flynn of Waterford, quoted in Brendan Fullam, *Hurling Giants* (1994).

'If the GAA feel genuinely embarrassed about the public cynicism which greets their big-match draws, someone had better organise an automatic time-keeping system. As yesterday's Bank of Ireland All-Ireland football final simmered towards its denouement, referee Pat McEneaney blew for fulltime after 40 seconds added for stoppages.'

Seán Moran, *The Irish Times*.

'The recent tendency to make balls smaller and more bulletlike should be discouraged, and balls of a fixed minimum weight and circumference should be encouraged.'

P.D. Mehigan, *The Irish Times* (January 1930).

'The sight and sound of Croke Park's great nabobs expatiating on pitch dimensions, a topic obviously remote indeed from their competence, revives once more the ancient proverb:

"The further up the tree the monkey goes, the more you see of his arse."'

Kevin Cashman, *Sunday Independent.*

'Nobody ever proposed making GAA goals bigger. Not even Charlie Redmond.'

Website, 101 reasons why GAA is better than soccer.

'Time, gentlemen. So, some 50 years after the GAA got rid of the Bogue Clock, Seán McCague is in favour of re-introducing some sort of time-keeping which should take that burden off the unfortunate, overburdened referee. Trouble is that Seán McCague has not informed us whether, or how, whatever system he has in mind is to be less hilarious than what we've endured for half a century.'

Kevin Cashman, *Sunday Independent.*

Views from Afar

Not everybody is able to get what the GAA is about or what it is up to. Some have their own peculiar views that it is a somewhat sinister nefarious organisation, trying to subvert their culture and destroy their values. If you come from one of those counties whose hearts are broken year after year by the prospect of not winning anything, you might be inclined to agree.

'I'm always suspicious of games where you're the only ones that play it.'
Jack Charlton, on hurling.

'It seems a strange game to me. When I listen to Michael McGee and Charlie Collins doing commentary they talk about the square ball, the breaking ball, the high ball and the low ball. They also talk about the player who got on his bike, then we had the one who cut through the defence like a knife through butter, and I would be worried about the player who ate the other one for his dinner (how would you like to be marking him). On top of all that the poor old referee never meets with their approval. Mind you I'm not surprised that he gets it wrong with all the different types of ball on the pitch, not to mention players on bicycles, others carrying knives to cut through butter. Is it any wonder I don't go to GAA matches. I'm confused enough after 30 years in soccer.'

Patsy McGowan, Finn Harps soccer manager.

"What's wrong with the GAA, that they won't let soccer or rugby at Croker? It's hardly any more foreign than Neil Diamond or American bore-ball, surely Paul McGrath or Mick Galwey have as much right to play there as our Yankee brothers.'

Christy Moore, singer.

'I enjoyed the Gaelic and I still go and watch as many matches as I can... These days, of course, Armagh don't seem to progress very far in the Ulster championship, it's no longer the Joe Kernan era! But it's such a strong part of the community in which I grew up and only the fact that I showed promise at the soccer and could make a living out of it, I suppose, took me away from it. I still look out for Armagh's results. Whenever they beat Derry, which hasn't been too regularly recently, I am not slow to let the gaffer know about it!'

Neil Lennon, soccer player with Glasgow Celtic.

'John McAuley, who has since gone to meet his Maker, and the Council took a decision not to include any reference on its then monthly calendar of events. The local All Saints GAA Club took the issue to the Northern Ireland Ombudsman. The ruling came out in favour of the GAA. The Council was found guilty of discrimination. It was the first, and last, time that refusing to publicise a game of football and the admission fee to a dance led to a Council being pilloried and fined. Stubborn to the end the Council decided to scrap the calendar of events rather than publish Irish words on Council documents.'

Terry McLaughlin, *Sunday Independent* (13 October 2002).

'Does the GAA take its democratic principles from the Tammany Hall school of democratic politics, or that former great bastion of democracy, the Soviet Communist Party?'

Letter to *The Irish Times* (14 April 2001).

'The evolution of the GAA was not a narrow pursuit in sporting Anglophobia but Irish sport embracing the British model of sport codification and mirroring the European, African, and Asian trend of ball games becoming an important part of the social fabric.'

Diarmaid Ferriter, *Transforming Ireland* (2004).

'The GAA mucksavages are anxious for their primal fix. You watch GAA matches, with all their brutality and innate stupidity. The type of tribal bestiality which they mistakenly call sport. The natural affinity with violence which is the trademark of Bogball.'

Declan Lynch, *Hot Press* (August 1993).

'The victory of Armagh was not a matter of rejoicing for those of that mindset. It was the opposite. It delivered a message of fear and isolation and separateness. The reality for the GAA is that for all its slick marketing and magnificent new stadia and high media profile, there are elected representatives in the North that firmly believe that the GAA, to quote one DUP Councillor, has not abandoned its sectarian and anti-Protestant bias.'

Terry McLaughlin (13 October 2002).

'Fenian control was more overt in the case of the GAA, but a clericalist faction led by Archbishop Croke remained active after 1887.'

David Fitzpatrick, Trinity College academic, in Roy Foster (ed.), *Oxford Illustrated History of Ireland* (2000).

'Gaelic football probably owed much to the popularity of rugby, in which early leading figures such as Michael Cusack and clubs, such as Laurne Rangers [sic] had previously been involved.'

Neal Garnham, in S.J. Connolly (ed.) *Oxford Companion to Irish History* (2004).

'It's time for the GAA to stop living in the past and make Croke Park available for competitive matches. I can understand them wanting to protect their own games, but the fact of the matter is that since 1988, even hardcore Gaelic fans have followed the Irish football team.'

Paul McGrath, footballer (7 February 2002).

'Hurling is alien to most Irish people too: we just like to pretend that it's our national pastime, when in real life our national pastime is perhaps more mundane. It consists of watching football on TV, several times a week if we possibly can, at home or in the pub, irrespective of who's playing, or the importance of the fixture.'

Declan Lynch, *Hot Press* (17 August 2003).

'GAA games elevate man-marking and strength over skill. The tactics involved, such as they are, are limited. The range of skills in soccer is far wider and the skills are more difficult to master.'

Diarmuid Doyle, *SundayTribune*.

'They are all smelly knackers from the bogs anyway. So regardless who won it does not really matter. Because the simple fact of the matter is that people from Dublin are just better than them. They know it and we certainly know it. End of story.'

Weblog, Deadparrots.com.

'The GAA decision not to permit a soccer fundraiser on its Omagh pitch bears out Erich Fromm's view that love for one's country which is not part of one's love for humanity is not love, but idolatrous worship.'

Letter to *The Irish Times* (15 September 1998).

County by County

Antrim

'It's the greatest day in Antrim's history.'
Jim Nelson, Antrim's hurling manager from the 1980s, after
the 1989 victory over Offaly.

'The worst thing about Antrim's exit was that we may never
see Cloot again in Croke Park. That, if it happens, is sad for
the rest of us. But nobody should worry about The Happy
Hurler himself. You may rest assured that he'll become the
champion at darts or croquet or skinydipping or something,
while you and I are still trying to master the elements of
beggar-my-neighbour.'
Kevin Cashman, *Sunday Independent* (15 August 1993).

'As a player I was a bad loser myself. A terrible bad loser. You
trained to be the best player and to win.'
Dinny Cahill of Antrim.

'Antrim has produced in recent years some fine scoring men
who can dribble trickily and drive beautifully.'
Dick Fitzgerald, *How to Play Gaelic Football* (1914).

Armagh

'They've suffered, these people, they suffered so much over the past years. This is their just reward.'

Joe Kernan, Armagh 2002 football manager.

'Am not gonna keep yous that long. I wish I had the words of 130 years of frustration. You don't need words to look down and see the sea of orange and white in front of me.'

Kieran McGeeney, Armagh 2002 football captain.

'When somebody tells you all your life that something is beyond your reach, that it's impossible, that you'll never get there, and then you do, well – there's that feeling that the work and toil that you put yourself through for 13 or 14 years has all come to fruition.'

Kieran McGeeney, Armagh 2002 football captain.

'Three years ago, Armagh came and splashed an orange innocence around Clones, winning an Ulster title that made a good season wonderful, the same group of players did a professional job on a young Donegal team and went through the celebratory motions. But it wasn't the same.'

Keith Duggan, *The Irish Times*.

'Kieran McGeeney, the Armagh captain, was an awesome character, approachable and articulate with a purity of passion unpolluted by money or agents or all the considerations of a professional life.'

Tom Humphries, *Laptop Dancing and the Nanny-Goat Mambo* (2003).

'I went from being a quiz question to a statistic.'
Jimmy Smyth, 1977 Armagh captain, on the side's 2002
victory.

'Thank God it's over, it was terrible to watch.'
Armagh fan, email to the BBC after 2002 All-Ireland final.

Carlow

'In weaker counties players are trying to talk themselves up,
that they are as good as the opposition, while subconsciously
they don't believe it.'
Cyril Hughes, former Carlow manager.

'Players are asked to be beware of their so called admirers
during the weekend.'
Carlow Nationalist preview of 1913 Leinster junior football
final.

'Players are training to get past the first round, not training to
win a Leinster final.'
Cyril Hughes, former Carlow manager.

'What a change in the last half did the minutes unroll/The
boys from the Barrow were swarming the goal/It was blue in
and odd spot, but red, gold an green./Were the colours that
rallied the Carlow fifteen.'
Ballad of Carlow's victory in the 1944 Leinster championship,
the county's only senior success.

Cavan

'Cavan were dead slow. You can't cut finished footballers out of a hedge. Muscle in the county is running wild for want of cultivation. Our players have no style, a clumsy catch and awkward delivery.'

Anglo Celt (1910).

'They only sold four programmes, one for each stand.'

Dessie Cahill, RTÉ broadcaster, recounting Cavan jokes after the 1997 All-Ireland semi-final.

Clare

'Hardly a Clare game has gone by in the last five years without some controversy arising. Should the GAA put an asterisk beside the 1998 record books: Winners Offaly: Clare gave great entertainment and made loads of money for the GAA?'

Letter to the *Irish Examiner* (4 September 1999).

'Clare had a team worthy of winning an All-Ireland in every decade but they weren't able to get there.'

Jimmy Smyth of Clare, quoted in Colm Keane, *Hurling's Top Twenty* (2002).

'In the past, even the language of the supporters carried the wail and the woe of what was said and unsaid. I hated the question "Will ye win?" People knew the answer to the question when they asked you. What they were saying was: "We want you to win, we know you can, but you won't."...

It's strange, but I felt more peace than euphoria when we won in '95. It was a fairy wand that cast a spell of happiness and contentment over the county and it's people at home and abroad. It was more than self-fulfillment, more than seeing the net shaking and more than the exuberance of health and fitness. It was on a plane far higher than this.'

Jimmy Smyth, Clare hurler from the 1950s, quoted in John Scally, *Raising the Banner* (2001).

'Clare pissed people off because they didn't conveniently feck off back to Doolin after 1995 and play their music till kingdom come.'

Anthony Daly, quoted by Enda McEvoy, *Sunday Tribune* (June 2000).

'Maybe the notion of fitness occurred to them about, say, once in every leap year. But, in those days before the first round of the Munster championship of 1995, when Banner men were being flayed up and down the sides of mountains, it was about Will you? Dare you? Trample on the toes of the people of Tipperary and Cork, as generations before you failed to do? And somewhere on those mountainsides Loughnane's men said yes, and gave us four or five years of hurling ecstasy.'

Kevin Cashman, *Sunday Independent.*

'The greatest moment of my life. It's something you cannot explain. All the frustrations, all the disappointments and all the walking home in sorrow were put aside. We no longer remembered the past. We remembered the present.'

Jimmy Smyth, Clare hurler from the 1950s, on the 1995 All-Ireland final.

'We celebrated that final like an All-Ireland. The Oireachtas was considered bigger than the league at the time.'

Jimmy Smyth, on Clare's victory in the 1954 Oireachtas final.

Cork

'Historically, Cork are probably the only County Board that has held both hurling and football in equal esteem to the mutual benefit of both games.'

Denis Flaherty, Kerry hurling selector.

'Try that again and there will be a by-election.'

Tony Reddan, Tipperary goalkeeper, talking to Jack Lynch after Lynch was elected to the Dáil while still a Cork hurler.

'Santy.'

Setanta Ó hAilpín's nickname in WIT.

'Carlos Santana.'

Setanta Ó hAilpín's nickname at Carlton Australian Rules club.

'I love Cork so much that if I caught one of their hurlers in bed with my missus, I'd tiptoe downstairs and make him a cup of tea.'

Joe Lynch, actor.

'From Three Stripe international to the Sonia gear row in Atlanta to Roy's rage over the training gear in Saipan (v-necked!!!) to the current leisure shirt crisis among the county hurlers there seems to be a Corkonian allergy to the basic fabrics of society. They do things different there. Cork once got a Munster hurling championship game postponed on account of a tall ships race. Cork, after all, are the people who took the train home from a big game in Croke Park rather than play extra-time.'

Tom Humphries, *The Irish Times* (2 December 2002).

'The finest side of skilled ashmen yet seen by the GAA.'

P.D. Mehigan, on the 1903 Cork hurling team.

'I went to a bus queue near Kenilworth Square. Several buses passed and there was a big queue and I was getting a bit worried. I was looking at my watch. After a while I got really worried I broke the queue and stepped on the platform of the bus. The bus conductor put up his hand. "Oh, nothing doing, you have to take your turn." I said, "Listen, I am playing in an All-Ireland final today." "Ah," he said, "that's the best one I have ever heard."'

Jack Lynch in conversation with Mick Dunne, quoted in Colm Keane, *Hurling's Top Twenty* (2002).

'Ger Loughnane merely articulated what most GAA people already know. When Cork oppose a proposal it is the equivalent of Moby Dick opposing a dinghy. Best not to get your hopes up.'

Vincent Hogan, *Irish Independent.*

'Hurling needed Limerick and Cork to set the standard for this championship, and that's what they did. A fantastic game, the best I've seen in the championship for some years. I know Limerick won, but the most memorable moment of the game – and may prove to be of the championship – was Diarmuid O'Sullivan's second-half point. That score on its own was worth the entry fee to this game. It didn't just lift the Cork team, it lifted the whole stand.'

Jimmy Barry Murphy, *Irish Examiner*.

'What's the world coming to? For over 70 years, no visiting county won at Páirc Uí Chaoimh. Now it's Cork that can't win there.'

Seán Moran, *The Irish Times*.

'My greatest memories were our games against Limerick in particular, who were almost at the peak of their best in those days. I always remember many a tussle I had with Mick Mackey.'

Jack Lynch, in conversation with Mick Dunne, quoted in Colm Keane, *Hurling's Top Twenty* (2002).

'I said, "I ought to play in Croke Park and I don't think I will play with the civil service." She said, even though she wasn't a typical GAA person, "Well surely your club comes first?" And I said, "Goodness you're right." I went out to Island-bridge and they asked me if I was going to play and I asked would they mind if I played in goal. I played in goal in the first half. There were three goals, one point and one wide in the first half. I decided it was time to give up any aspirations I might have to be a goalkeeper. We had no tracksuits in those days except to pull up my trousers over my togs and dash to Croke Park, just change jerseys and go out with Munster. I remember well a ball coming across towards the end of the second game and we were about a point or two down. Somebody passed it to me and I was coming in. I had to run fairly fast to get it, but I hadn't the energy to kick it. If I had it would have been an easy goal.'

Jack Lynch, in conversation with Mick Dunne, quoted in Colm Keane, *Hurling's Top Twenty* (2002).

'Things are easier in Clare and Tipperary and Galway and Kilkenny, startling though that assertion may sound. Sociologists of all shades, and none, blame JBM and Johnny Clifford and The Canon and anyone you care to nominate for Cork's failure to win more then two All-Irelands in the '90s. The world and Katty Barry ought to know that neither Jimmy, nor Frank, nor Con, nor The Doc nor any other Murphy who ever lived could have reversed, or even affected, that law of the Celtic Tiger which dictates that a family shall consist of 1.8326 persons. When Cork hurling was great, a northside family consisted of eight persons – and counting.'

Kevin Cashman, *Sunday Independent.*

'Rebels without a pause.'

Irish Independent headline, on the runaway Cork victory over Waterford (1982).

'I often passed scores of fellows on the road from Cork to Limerick, and Cork to Thurles, and when I was living in Dublin, from Dublin to Thurles. A funny thing in those days was that participants were entitled to travel in a taxi but nobody else. I remember driving from Dublin to Thurles in a taxi all by myself and some of my friends, my colleagues on the civil service hurling team, many of them Cork people, were cycling. I passed some of them around Portlaoise and there I was sitting in my glory. It was a silly thing.'

Jack Lynch, in conversation with Mick Dunne, quoted in Colm Keane, *Hurling's Top Twenty* (2002).

'That was the day our youngsters became men.'

Jimmy Barry Murphy, on the 1999 Cork vs Clare match.

Derry

'McGurk was about to enter into folklore. He is reputed to have sold the magic left boot at a couple of dozen impromptu auctions in the US. Over and over again.'

Tom Humphries, *The Irish Times*.

'Is this in recognition of all the one-parent families on the present panel?'

Joe Brolly, Derry footballer from the 1990s, questioning a Derry county board official when the team received only one complimentary ticket prior to their 1998 Ulster semi-final.

'I remember at half-time seeing Coleman and thinking that he was resigned to it. The game was lost. Mickey just lost his temper. He shouted and roared. He could see that we could do it. He could sense the Dublin defence was flakey.'

Joe Brolly, Derry footballer from the 1990s.

'At half-time Eamon was nearly dead on his feet. He did his wee bit but you could see he thought we were in bother. And then suddenly Mickey Moran took things by the scruff of the neck. Mickey gave the bit of inspiration. He said very little usually. Eamonn was always the motivator. Mickey was just on fire that day. Even for me. I went in disappointed and came out all fired up. Just sitting on the bench thinking that we'd win it. The second-half performance was the best half hour we played as a team.'

Danny Quinn, Derry footballer from the 1990s, on the 1993 All-Ireland final.

'The old Croke Park had more atmosphere. The place was heaving. In the second half you couldn't hear anything. Just roaring and screaming. The last 10, 15 minutes just people screaming. It must have been a terribly exciting match. I remember in The Hill one of the Dubs had a blow-up doll and as the game went on the doll began to sag. I meant to look to see how she was at the end.'

Joe Brolly, Derry footballer from the 1990s.

'There's always that problem when you get Brolly involved. That was a bit of crack. I still have the boot. What Brolly never says is how he got the boot he scored his point with sprayed gold for his mantelpiece. I have the boot and I have Pat Gilroy's jersey. He gave it to me and I suppose he thought I was entitled to it – I'd been grabbing it all day long.'

John McGurk, Derry footballer from the 1990s.

'Tony Davis cods me these days if he hadn't been sent off Cork would have won. We felt it was inevitable. The big game was the semi-final. The dressing room for the final was completely different. We were quiet and tense before we went out. We knew what we were going to do.'

Joe Brolly, Derry footballer from the 1990s.

'Better executives than Clare's would have demanded that they carry their three-point lead into the third leg; better sportsmen than Offaly – after the glorious success of their sit-in – would have suggested without prompting that Clare's lead stand. (Isn't it the quare phenomenon that the strategy of the sit-in didn't even occur to the Gaelic football folk of Derry when their minors were done down, short weeks since? Where was Eamonn McCann and Neil McCafferty when they were needed?)'

Kevin Cashman, writing prior to 1998 All-Ireland senior hurling final, *Sunday Independent.*

'Seeing the Hill. Seeing those sky-blue shirts. The place stuffed. Hill 16 all Dublin. Their supporters are unbelievable. I loved it.'

Tony Scullion, on the 1993 All-Ireland semi-final.

Donegal

'What we needed was to lose the fear of winning, not the fear of losing.'

Brian McEniff, Donegal manager, on his county's victory in 1992.

'Donegal is a strange county. It is a stretch of untameable landscape inhabited by very diverse towns. Bundoran, a seaside resort of clubs and surfers where Brian McEniff, the 1992 manager comes from, has nothing at all in common with Ardara, the picturesque arts-and-crafts community and the home of Anthony Molloy, the only Donegal man to lift the Sam Maguire. And Inishowen is a world away from the robust

and prosperous fishing town of Killybegs. To Bloody Foreland people, Donegal town might well be in Connacht. Some would tell you it is.'
Keith Duggan, *The Irish Times* (3 August 2002).

Down

Newspaper headline during 1963 Cuban missile crisis: 'Kruschev Backs Down.'

Down supporter: 'Why wouldn't he, aren't they going to win?'
Quoted in Tommy Sands, *The Song Man* (2005).

Dublin

'Mick Holden was a hurler on his holidays from football.'
Tom Humphries, *The Irish Times*.

'Some viewers might find this upsetting – so look away now.'
Michael Lyster, talking before he replayed Dessie Farrell's miss against Kerry (2002).

'No comment, and by the way, you can't quote me.'
Brian Mullins, the notoriously media-unfriendly Dublin footballer from the 1970s and 1980s.

'How dare Dr Pat O'Neill assert that Dublin GAA was or is tribal (Sport, October 20th) when it has always been open, multicultural and cosmopolitan? That said, one thing is sure:

the Dubs don't need culchies telling them how to play football.'

Letter to *The Irish Times* (November 2004).

'It was a magnificent achievement to hit the crossbar, if you tried all afternoon you wouldn't do it again – and Dessie's the best of their forwards.'

Pat Spillane, on the same miss (2002).

'This fifteen representing Dublin in 1927 are the best I have ever seen.'

P.D. Mehigan, *The Irish Times*.

'It is only a matter of time before Dublin GAA reflects the multi-racial presence in the city. In decades or less, an entire half-back line might have its origins in three continents when once a southsider in the ranks would have appeared as nothing short of exotic.'

Keith Duggan, *The Irish Times* (3 August 2002).

'It was surprised it hit the post because it looked like it was going three foot wide.'

Tommy Lyons, on Ray Cosgrove's 2002 would-be equaliser against Armagh.

'Jayo is at once a representative of the future and an emblem of the recent but already fading past. He was, in the truest sense of the word, a sensation – half charisma, half media overkill. Truth is, he is no longer the kid he was – Jayo's a father now – and is happy to concentrate on kicking points. He still has vehement critics of his skill as a Gaelic footballer, people who see him as a lightweight waste of a good jersey. Others argue that the subtle immensity of his contribution to 1995 was overlooked in both that year's All Star scheme and by those who claim he is dispensable.'

Keith Duggan, on Dublin footballer Jason Sherlock, *The Irish Times*.

'We knew the GAA wanted Dublin to win an All-Ireland but he hadn't realised they wanted it that badly.'

Art McRory, Tyrone manager, after Tyrone were beaten by Dublin in the 1995 All-Ireland football final.

'No defeat as a manager ever hit me like 1955. That was the first time there. It was Kerry. I had great hopes and so on and so on. That formed a large part of what I became as a person.'

Kevin Heffernan, on the 1955 All-Ireland final.

'The tone of the previews of that September's All-Ireland final was the argument that Dublin "deserved" an All-Ireland even before a ball was kicked.'

Danny Murphy, Down chairman, in the 1994 Down yearbook.

'Dublin are a streak team, and when they succeed in building up a head of steam, they are quite an outfit.'

Mick O'Dwyer, *Irish Examiner*.

'Like it or not, the capital is essential to the well-being of the GAA. Dublin's arrival in the mid-1970s did give the GAA a nationwide profile. Without a presence in the city, the association could hardly consider itself national. Dublin's success is always a useful focus for the rest of the country and the contribution made by the county to the evolution of the modern GAA is considerable.'

Seán Moran (30 June 1999).

'So cute. Very calming. He has a bigger influence on the game than people understand.'

Tommy Lyons, on Dessie Farrell (30 June 2003).

'The feeling the Heffernan years invoked – that tremulous awakening – cannot be revisited. And perhaps part of the problem for Dublin football is that its players feel in a vague way obliged to evoke that era again. Instead, they just borrow its brightest tools.'

Keith Duggan (12 June 2004).

'When we're good, we're the best in the world, and when we're bad, we're the worst in the world.'

Dave Billings, manager from the 1990s, on Dublin fans.

'Under new guidelines the GAA have issued a new rule. In the event of the match being level after seventy minutes Dublin will win.'

Weblog.

'The first ball I got I ran at him. He didn't foul me really but he had a free given against him. So the next ball I ran at him again and he hesitated because he had been blown for the first one. That was fatal. That started the rot. Dublin humiliated Meath that day.'

Kevin Heffernan, on his performance against Paddy O'Brien in 1955 Leinster championship.

'Hill 8?'

Con Houlihan, in a letter to *The Irish Times*, on a proposal that Dublin should field two county teams.

Fermanagh

'Fermanagh has such a small playing base. Half the county is made up of water and half of the remaining half are Protestants.'

Dessie Cahill, RTÉ broadcaster.

Galway

'A mhuintir na Gaillimhe: tar éis seacht mbliain agus caoga, tá craobh na hÉireann ar ais I nGallaimh. Tá daoine ar ais i nGallaimh agus tá gliondar ina gcroí. Ach freisin caithfimid cuimhne ar daoine i Sasana I Mericea ar fud na tire agus tá siad ag caoineadh anois láthair.'

Joe Connolly, giving his victory speech after Galway had won the 1980 All-Ireland hurling championship, widely regarded as the best in GAA history.

'It amuses me when I hear of teams training first thing in the morning as if it was something brand new. Galway were doing that and more in the 1980s.'

Pete Finnerty, Galway hurler from the 1980s.

'It was a scoreline that the Meath supporters could scarcely believe. Given their team's performances during the year, they felt the only way the Green and Gold could be denied was by equipping the opposition with silver bullets and starting the match at midnight.'

Miriam Lord, *Irish Independent.*

'The sort of football played by Galway in the second-half of Sunday's final will always pay dividends. It was based on honest hard work, great teamwork and fearless determination to give everything you have for the honour and glory of your native county. So long as those attitudes survive Gaelic football has not too much to fear.'

Eugene McGee, *Irish Independent.*

'As you do unto others, so shall it be done unto you. The matador sound effects with which Meath supporters had taunted Kerry a brief three weeks before were turned against them as a stylish and convincing Galway team elegantly played down the clock after an extraordinary end to what has been an historic Bank of Ireland football championship.'

Seán Moran, *The Irish Times.*

'How many times did you read, or hear over the airwaves, that Galway had "a new team"? In fact, Galway had just three new players; and of those only Murt Killilea could be accounted "new" in the real sense of the word: Padraic Kelly and Joe McGrath were, or should have been, at the head of every notebook that ever got anywhere near a Sarsfields match – and they're the All-Ireland club champions.'

Kevin Cashman, *Sunday Independent* (15 August 1993).

'Joe Rabbitte, in particular, can harbour some justifiable complaints about the referee's interpretation of his attacking style.

Rabbitte's path to goal was repeatedly blocked by a massed Tipperary defence, but, more often than not, the call went against the forward, even on occasions when he looked to be more sinned against than sinning.'

Martin Breheny, *Irish Independent.*

'Padraic Joyce is a class act, and the Galway full-forward joined the game's immortals with his 10-point scoring feat which adorned Sunday's All-Ireland football final and sent Meath reeling.'

Cliona Foley, *Irish Independent.*

'Over the Maroon.'

Irish Mirror headline, on the celebrations surrounding the victorious 2000 Galway football team as it returned home.

Kerry

'He was a man-mountain, he could catch aeroplanes if it helped Kerry.'

John B. Keane, on Mick O'Connell, the Kerry footballer from the 1960s.

'Mick O'Connell. I remember once hearing about how he had jumped so high to make a catch, that his boots tripped over his opponents shoulders.'

Gerry McGovern, *Hot Press* (25 August 1993).

'County colours have become so flamboyantly fashionable that it's only a matter of time before John Rocha designs an

entire capsule collection around the concept of championship chic. He'll probably skip the Kerry colours. Even a
designer of Mr Rocha's noted abilities would struggle to
create a flattering ensemble out of that sow's ear. Our bracing
combination of glaring green and gaudy gold breaks every
rule in the Colour Me Beautiful rulebook.'

The Kerryman (28 August 2003).

'We just felt that because the Mayo inside-forwards are small,
maybe their backs would not be all that used to high ball
coming in at training. We decided to check it out.'

Jack O'Connor, Kerry manager, revealing the masterstroke
behind his side's victory (2004).

'Most backs are happy enough if they've marked their own
man and won the ball that came their way, Séamus is different. He's always looking to take a pass from a team-mate
who's under pressure or to cover for someone else. He's
hungry for the ball all the time.'

Darren Fay, on Kerry full-back Seamus Moynihan.

'If Kerry lose either the manager was to blame or the players
were to blame. There's no such thing as you were beaten by
the better team.'

Páidí Ó Sé, quoted in Colm Keane, *A Cut Above the Rest*
(1999).

'Year after year went by, the winters became longer and
longer. Nothing changed in the real world: the sun rose and
went down; the cows gave their milk; the rooks went off in
the morning and came home in the evening. Life, however,

was not normal in Kerry; small lads and small ladies graduated from primary school without seeing the Golden Fleece come to the county.'

Con Houlihan (21 September 2003).

'When Kerry have won a game, the pub talk on the morrow is muted: there is a glow of satisfaction that needs little articulation. When, however, Kerry have lost, it is rather different: the search is on for scapegoats, not to mention scapesheep and scapeasses.'

Con Houlihan.

'T'would be nice, Páidí, t'would be nice.'

John Egan, giving his serene response to a query from Páidí Ó Sé before a big game, 'I suppose you'll be sticking in a few today?'

'How could a very good team, a side in search of greatness, a team with All Stars in every line, be annihilated like this?'

Diarmuid O'Flynn, on Kerry's defeat to Meath in the 2001 All-Ireland semi-final, *Irish Examiner*.

'Maybe it's time to reappraise the notion that Kerry and Meath are the kingpins of Gaelic football.'

Mick O'Dwyer, after the 2001 All-Ireland semi-final, *Irish Examiner*.

'My old friend Jackie Lyne had his own theory about Kerry's pre-eminence. With those bastards of mountains behind and that whore of an ocean in front, we have to do something.'

Con Houlihan (21 September 2003).

'If we never won another match this would keep me going.'
Maurice Leahy, Kerry hurling selector, after Kerry's win over
Waterford (1993).

'What's Wrong With Our Football?'
The Kerryman (1959).

'If he'd done it in training in front of two blackbirds and a
Jack Russell it'd still have been marvellous, but in injury time
in an All-Ireland quarter-final with the words "Your County
Needs You" ringing in his ears? Inconceivable. Next time you
bump in to Maurice Fitzgerald genuflect.'
Mary Hannigan, on Maurice Fitzgerald's last-minute point in
the 2001 All-Ireland football quarter-final, *The Irish Times*.

Kildare

Eamonn O'Donoghue, Kildare manager: 'Who's gonna win this
match?'

Player: 'At this stage, Eamonn, you'd nearly have to fancy the
Dubs.'
Conversation at half-time in the 1978 Leinster final.

'There was slight rumblings in Kildare amongst a few hardcore though not hard up for cash GAA fans, when their
beloved serpent was airbrushed out of their county crest.
Some fans were of the opinion that the serpent in the crest
gave the county a bit more menace – and God knows they
could do with a bit of that in the shortgrass county, especially
when coming up against the likes of the hard chaw Jackeens

or the wild mucksavages from Meath. Just being a Lillywhite is hardly enough to strike the fear of God into the heart of those hoors.'

Sheepstealers.com, Roscommon fans' website.

'This is a Kildare team that never know when to stop running... if the people of this country don't like the brand of football we play, then I'm sorry for them.'

Mick O'Dwyer, speaking after Kildare's defeat of Dublin (2002).

'After training we went back to a house for tea and you had to fight with the dog for the sandwiches.'

Pat Dunney, on Kildare training in the 1970s.

'In Germany, you don't mention the war – in Kildare, you don't mention the wides.'

Damian Lawlor, *The Star*.

'Good performance by Dublin, they're against a woeful and inept opposition, an inept opposition where a forward line, not one of them could manage to score from play... but, of course, what's new with Kildare forwards? A team who continue to short-pass the ball, who take eight passes to get to the 50 yard line, a team who overcarry the ball. Christ, they're a team who are so easy to defend against!'

Pat Spillane, on Kildare (2002).

'Me no worry, me no care, Me play football with Kildare, Micko says you tall and thin. You take place of Ronan Quinn. Micko is a clever man, He watch me play in Pakistan, Basketball is my game, Micko say it all the same, Me pack bag and head for Naas, Jar of tippex in my case, Go on labour, sign on dole, Next week get money, so me tole. Me train hard for this big game, Get to know the other's name, There's men from Kerry, Cork and Tipp, Roscommon too and Leixlip. We got Galway in our sights They no beat the Silly Whites. Micko has us all on fire, But who the ***** is Sam Maguire.'

Packie White, Kildare bard.

'With Tipperary's Brian Lacey, Cork man Brian Murphy O'Dwyers son Karl and Meath's Cathal Sheridan all playing prominent roles in recent years, Kildare have become the inter-county equivalent of a League of Nations.'

Colm Coyle, former Meath footballer.

Kilkenny

'Cat Food.'

Irish Independent headline, after Kilkenny's demolition of Offaly (2001).

'He might make the team of the next millennium instead.'

Michael Lyster of RTÉ, when D.J. Carey was not selected on the hurling team of the millennium (2001).

'Kilkenny had a new trainer, a young priest called Fr Tommy Maher who, well aware of the favourites' power in the air, coached his team to play the ball low and not give their opponents any time to stand over the sliotar and pick it up. Kilkenny won by 6–9 to 1–5 on an afternoon that Wexford's greatest team perished and the foundation stone of modern hurling's empire of empires was laid.'

Enda McEvoy, *Sunday Tribune* (20 June 2004).

'Who's on the stamp? D.J.'s on the stamp.'

Banner, welcoming D.J. Carey back to Kilkenny after the 2000 All-Ireland final, when D.J. was excluded from the team of the millennium.

'There were 15 better hurlers in the game over the past century; I haven't seen any of them. I am now officially putting Carey in as captain of the new millennium team.'

Peter Finnerty, *Sunday Independent* (2001).

'Kilkenny are the luckiest team in Ireland today or any other day.'

Tom Semple of Tipperary, after the 1912 All-Ireland final.

'But soft, what light from yonder window breaks? It is the east, and Fr John Joe Reidy is the sun.'

Enda McEvoy, *Fennessy's Field: A Century of Hurling History at St Kieran's College, Kilkenny.*

'Carrying a wand which resembled a hurling stick, he looked like a man who could gallop across water without causing a ripple on the surface.'

Colm O'Rourke, on D.J. Carey, *Sunday Independent* (2001).

'Will e'er a television set in the entire land survive dear Liam's convulsions if Carey ever scores a goal remotely approaching the virtuosity of English's kick in '87, or Foxy's flick in '91, or Fenton's whip in '87, or Barry Murphy's deathless double in

'83? D.J. Carey is quite a good player. He is not, was not, the greatest hurler of all time nor even of the decade he inhabited. Joe Cooney, John Leahy, Brian Whelahan, Ciarán Carey and Mark Foley beside him, Brian Lohan, Brian Corcoran, Declan Ryan were the best hurlers of the '90s; and if you had to go to the Alamo or the GPO you'd want Michael Coleman and Martin Storey along.'

Kevin Cashman, *Sunday Independent* (15 August 1993).

'When this century is a little more jaded – when we can isolate our Gaelic stars on Playercam – we will probably have a more settled perspective on the brilliance of the current Kilkenny full-forward line.'

Seán Moran, *The Irish Times*.

'He was Hurler of the Year with nobody close enough to claim they were second.'

Denis Walsh, on Henry Shefflin's 2002 award.

'I haven't seen anything as good in 10 years, they gave up four points and scored 3–9.'

Ger Loughnane, on the Kilkenny vs Tipperary 2003 All-Ireland semi-final.

'All their talk. They have no All-Irelands. We have two All-Irelands. When they learn how to win All-Irelands they can talk.'

John Leahy, on Galway after the 1994 league final.

'John Power, he kept coming back. He never stopped. Next ball you could be damn sure he'd be going for it. He was fierce strong and honest as well. He used to get it, but by Jesus he was able to give it back as well.'

Liam Dunne, the Wexford hurler, on John Power.

'I said to Joe Brady, "You go in centre-back." I don't think he knew that it was me making the switch and not the sideline but it didn't matter, I wasn't staying there any longer.'

Brian Whelahan, on marking Henry Shefflin (2002).

'4–7–11 – what a stinker!'

Kilkenny People headline, taken from the number of players who turned up at training sessions for the county football team.

Laois

'Whether any of the Laois messengers bothered to explain some of the facts of life regarding Laois football to Micko is something we do not know but sure he will soon find out for himself the sort of internal club wrangling and self-inflicted wounds that have played a large part in the demise of Laois as a serious football force.'

Eugene McGee, *Irish Independent* (20 September 2002).

'Sometimes I used to think to myself that I wasn't supposed to win.'

Martin Cuddy of Laois, quoted in Brendan Fullam, *Hurling Giants* (1994).

Leitrim

'Knowing that life isn't fair. That's the rule of Packie McGarty.'
Tom Humphries, *The Irish Times* (10 May 2003).

'Up Leitrim up Leitrim/They are the champions of the fight /Frank follows Heslin and Brennan/Morning noon and night /Heslin is the best/O'Beirne is the next/When they don't come round to Martins/Frank is very vexed.'
Gus Martin's first ever poem, composed as a child.

'Three teams terrified the life out of us. I still remember them, Aughnasheelin, Aughawilliam and Aughvass, would come down to play the Ballinamore lads, and strike terror into what was mostly a team of soft college boys. They would stare you down before even a ball was thrown in, and try to disable you with the first move of the match. We usually considered ourselves faster and fitter than them, but we weren't tougher than them.'
Gus Martin, *Irish Press* (15 August 1994).

Limerick

'Spirited and reckless, they were prepared to put their heads where another would not risk his hurley.'
Freeman's Journal, on the 1917 Limerick team.

'A lot of strong men can't use their strength. But Mick was very well put together and could use it. He mightn't be as good as hurling in the air as other fellows. But when he came down he could take it. He could throw fellows out of the way. He could do it in a very purposeful way. He could go up the middle. He never had to go up the sideline or anything like that. When he went with the solo runs he was a great man to finish them and score. He was a great match winner. He was a team by himself.'

Dick Stokes of Limerick, team-mate of Mick Mackey, quoted in Colm Keane, *Hurling's Top Twenty* (2002).

'You're in odd form today but you won't smell the next one.'

Mick Mackey, to Kilkenny goalkeeper Jimmy O'Connell after he made a save during 1940 All-Ireland hurling final, quoted in Breandán Ó hEithir, *Over the Bar* (1984).

'Mick Mackey always gave it tough and took it, and he'd hit you hard. If you were fool enough to be in the way, that was your business. There was a kind of smile on his face when he was doing these things.'

Jack Lynch, in conversation with Mick Dunne, quoted in Colm Keane, *Hurling's Top Twenty* (2002).

'He bought a pair of boots in Tyler's shop.'

Dick Stokes, talking about how John 'Tyler' Mackey got his nickname, quoted in Colm Keane, *Hurling's Top Twenty* (2002).

'It just happened.'

Ned Rea, talking about Limerick's victory in 1973.

'It's hard to beat the sense of caught breath at a championship match when a team is unexpectedly cresting the wave. It's harder still to beat the buzz that tingles around the ground when a match belatedly erupts into a contest. But it's hardest of all to beat three goals in six minutes.'

Seán Moran, after Limerick came from 11 points down to beat Waterford in 2001, *The Irish Times*.

'Kilkenny wouldn't have won had they had ten Eddie Kehers.'

Eamonn Grimes, Limerick hurler, on the 1973 All-Ireland hurling final.

'Not by much, but it went in a straight line all the way.'

Bernie Hartigan, talking about Richie Bennis' controversial winning point against Tipperary in 1973.

'It was the hottest day I ever hurled.'

Ciaran Carey, talking about the defeat of Clare in 1996, and that solo-run winning point, quoted in Brendan Fullam, *Legends of the Ash* (1997).

'They just fought and fought and fought. I stood on the side of the field with 15 minutes to go, pleading with them to take their points and the goals would follow. And the goals came.'

Eamonn Cregan, talking after Limerick came from 11 points down to beat Waterford in 2001.

'The Limerick half-back line was nicknamed the Hindenberg Line.'

Seán Óg Ó Ceallacháin, referee, *Tall Tales and Banter* (1998).

Long ford

'This time next year we'll take some beating. Remember this boat is only six months launched.'

Eamonn Coleman, Longford manager, after his adopted county ran Wicklow to a point in the 1996 Leinster championship.

'It changed my sporting philosophy forever. When Dublin drew level with twenty minutes remaining, a change came over my team: they became overwhelmed, they froze, they gave up, they looked like a team that had never trained together. I was astonished and baffled. What had happened? They were fit enough. They couldn't suddenly become less skilful, could they?'

Brendan Hackett, sports psychologist, on how Longford lost a 3-point half-time lead against Dublin and suffered defeat by 18 points in the 1988 Leinster championship.

Louth

'A county whose last All-Ireland winning team in '57 was captained by a 'champeen' accordion player. In fact, we can't exactly remember who played better that day, Dermot O'Brien or his accordion?'

Liam Cahill, An Fear Rua website (12 June 2000).

Mayo

'A lot of people felt I wasn't 100 per cent committed to Mayo football because I always played basketball. They are entitled to that opinion. But I reckon I'd be a wino on the streets now if I didn't play basketball. That's what kept me sane. I played in six All-Ireland football finals. Drew one and lost five. And that can take a lot out of a fella.'

Liam McHale.

'Well that's settled, the Mayo colours are red and green. Not so. The Mayo colours are the green above the red. God forbid that Mayo should ever have red above the green.'

Dick Walsh.

'The Mayo boys will be sitting in the dressing room like a big truck has run all over them, surveying the wreckage... the game's over, Kerry have destroyed them in every way.'

Joe Brolly, half-time speech in the 2004 All-Ireland final, in which Mayo were heavily defeated.

'I'm going home to burn this flag. It's just a complete waste of time following them.'

Mayo supporter, to RTÉ.

'The biggest sense of regret I would have is that we were so badly organised when I first came on to the county scene.'

Willie Joe Padden, Mayo footballer from the 1990s.

'Mayo are being courted by the Wide-Angle Lenses division of Kodak (get the picture, no matter how wide the shot is their famous slogan). Meath County Board have strenuously denied rumours of approaches by the National Lottery (We have draws every week).'

Weblog.

'Managing the Mayo footballers could be regarded as the ultimate test for any person in view of that county's record over the past 50 years. Once again there is a vacancy for the position and the county board has come up with the brilliant idea of appointing a 12-person committee to find a new Mayo manager. The idea seems to be that the more people out looking for a manager in Mayo the better chance there is of one being spotted.'

Eugene McGee (20 September 2002).

'Basically, Colm O'Rourke, we're looking at a murder scene.'

Michael Lyster, at half-time in the 2004 All-Ireland final.

'We'd have been quicker walking.'

Mayo official, talking about Mayo's decision to travel on Knock Airport's inaugural flight to London for their 1986 championship tie in Ruislip. The flight was delayed by bad weather and eventually diverted via Shannon.

Meath

'Meath players are decent, honest-to-God young men playing a particular brand of football which demands from them bravery and courage and ruthlessness.'

Liam Hayes (5 January 1997).

'There is no mystery about Meath football despite all the hype attached to it by some media people over the years. Meath players play with total commitment to their county's cause which should be the starting point for any set of county players. They mark tightly in defence, they tackle hard and fair. Their forwards get to the ball first and take their scores at the first available opportunity. They do not worry about kicking the ball wide. As a group the Meath players never worry about falling into serious arrears. They always have faith in themselves to come back. Now what is so mysterious about all that?'

Eugene McGee, *Irish Independent.*

'In this mood, Meath's defence is a startling union. You can practise 'til your head hurts and your hands bleed without ever approaching the kind of telepathy that keeps Cormac Sullivan's goal protected.'

Vincent Hogan, *Irish Independent.*

'Meath's midfield pair to leave Teddy bear.'

Banner at 1987 All-Ireland final.

'To me, the decline has come about because of a drop in standards of discipline and individual preparation on and off the field. No one should ever put on a Meath jersey who doesn't want to die for it.'

Gerry McEntee of Meath.

Monaghan

'It's pointless.'

Billy Morgan, the Cork manager, to Monaghan manager when asked about Kerry's weaknesses prior to the 1979 All-Ireland football semi-final.

'The Equaliser.'

Irish Independent headline, on Eamonn McEneaney after one of the most dramatic equalising points in football history (1985).

'We felt that we were on the outside of the fish bowl looking in.'

Eamonn McEneaney, Monaghan manager, on the success enjoyed by Ulster teams in the 1990s and 2000s.

'This bunch of boys have wore the shirt off their backs for Monaghan football.'

Eamonn McEneaney, Monaghan manager, after Monaghan won the 2005 Division Two title.

Offaly

'Liberté, egalité, we want un replé.'

Darragh McManus, on the 1998 Offaly sit-in that forced the Clare vs Offaly All-Ireland hurling semi-final to be replayed, *High Ball* (1998).

'Offaly yesterday found themselves facing not only the reigning champions: there was also the old husbands' tale that before being summoned to the round table you must already have been rebuffed at least once. And the "traditionalists" those amusing mystics who believe that it takes several generations to produce a hurler – looked on as Offaly's presence in the final as aficionados of the bullring might look on an Irish matador.'

Con Houlihan (September 1981).

'We're Offaly Sorry.'
Offaly banner at the 1981 All-Ireland final.

'What Offaly have in supreme measure is what we who can look back from the high hill of old age used to be startled by and terrified by when practised by Tipp's great team of half a century since: supernal "combination and teamwork" it was called then.'
Cork writer Kevin Cashman, *Sunday Independent.*

'You can say what you like, but this is a thoroughbred versus a dray horse.'
Fan, on the 1980 Leinster final Kilkenny vs Offaly.

'We always felt that we could beat Wexford. It was no different in 1996. They hadn't beaten us for nearly twenty years, but I suppose a bit of tiredness had crept into us at that stage. We had a few hard years behind us. My own firm belief is that Clare in 1995 and Wexford in 1996 were no fitter or better than any other year but they had the belief they could win from Loughnane and Griffin. We lost it on the line. For some unknown reason Michael Duignan was moved into the corner from midfield and I remember a big gap suddenly opened up on the Cusack Stand side of the field after half-time when they got four points in the first ten minutes. That gave them the belief and rhythm to go on and win it.'
Johnny Pilkington, Cork hurler from the 1990s.

'The events of Autumn 1998 had tainted the back door with a nasty dose of woodworm. Offaly were given the McCarthy Cup – they did not win it. They were beaten twice – by

Kilkenny and Clare – and, by the time they were presented with their place in the final, they still had not beaten Clare: the score at the end of the 207.5 minutes was 48 points apiece. Better executives than Clare's would have demanded that they carry their three-point lead into the third leg; better sportsmen than Offaly – after the glorious success of their sit-in – would have suggested without prompting that Clare's lead stand. The first decree of the Truth and Justice Commission, in this most distressful country, will render the 1998 championship null and void.'

Kevin Cashman, *Sunday Independent* (1998).

'If you hear anybody from Clare complaining, they don't represent Clare hurling.'

Ger Loughnane.

'It had to be done.'

Stephen Byrne, on his late save from Fergal Hegarty.

'Joe Quaid parried Johnny Dooley's penalty. Joe Dooley punched like a hawk on a chicken too far from his mother.'

Con Houlihan, *Evening Press* (September 1994).

'When Brian Whelahan was hurling well, I didn't think we could be beaten.'

Offaly team-mate of Brian Whelahan.

'Five pucks by Offaly were worth seven by Clare.'

Kevin Cashman, *Sunday Independent* (1998).

Roscommon

'A clean and interesting game with splashes of high football thrills and at times a little over keenness.'
Roscommon Champion, report on the 1943 All-Ireland final.

'I'm not saying we're the Brazillians of the West, but in summary I'd say the Rossies have thick hides wrapped around poetic souls, producing hard footballers who can turn on the style when needs be. And if our men ever fear venturing too far from our true hard chaw natures, we only need ask, "What Would Harry Keegan Do?", and we'll be set right again.'
Sheepstealers.com, the Roscommon fans' website.

'A Roscommon team is not a Roscommon team without at least two, big long midfielders who can jump into the sky and have a cup of tay and a sandwich while they're up there, along with a bit of a hatchet man in defence, producing a style of football that the outsider would be more apt to describe as the pragmatic sort.'
Sheepstealers.com, the Roscommon fans' website.

'The Roscommon man is a believer. He believes that the incoming year will be a mighty year for beef prices. He believes that Fianna Fáil will once again form a single-party government. He believes that it will be the best summer of his lifetime, illuminated by the best fishing season of all time. He believes that Roscommon will win the football All-Ireland. If you look closely into those blue eyes you will see a little hurt there. That lost hurt look is perhaps the Roscommon man's greatest possession. The Roscommon men make great Gaelic footballers when the pitch is heavy and the ball is played high. This is because of the build and keen sight. They won All-Ireland titles in the forties when the game of Gaelic football was the long ball and the high catch game. In later years the game has speeded up and there is infinitely more groundwork involved. For this reason Roscommon will never again win an All-Ireland. This adds yet another layer of hurt to the blue eyes.'

Cormac McConnell, writer.

'Poor, dear old Ros. Or Rosgommon, as true saffron-and-blue locals refer to it. It is so long since we won an All-Ireland. Fifty-four bleedin years. People like me have absolutely no idea what it is like to belong to a county which has won the Sam Maguire.'

Roscommon writer Patsy McGarry, *The Irish Times* (8 September 1998).

'Ah yes, the career of the Gaelic footballer can end in a flash. Just ask any Roscommon player.'

Keith Duggan, on an incident in which Roscommon players played pool in the nude, *The Irish Times* (2002).

'Downing Shorts.'

The Star has fun with Roscommon's naked pool players (2002).

Sligo

'The Sligo people are basically a very nice, quiet, reserved people and some of these youngsters, I can't even get them to shout for a ball loud at training. They're very soft-spoken.'
Mickey Moran, former Sligo manager (1999).

'We had fed the heart on fantasies.'
W.B. Yeats, quoted as an epithet for Sligo football by Brian Maye (18 July 2000).

'The fools. They've scored too early.'
Eamonn Sweeney, describing the fatalism of Sligo GAA supporters when they took a big lead in a 1998 championship match.

Tipperary

'But for the net it would have hit Blackrock Castle two miles away.'
P.D. Mehigan, on Tommy Treacy's goal for Tipperary against Limerick (1937).

'The crowd was on top of me in the second half and I was in the middle. With ten minutes left to go I got the ball and this blackcoat (fan) threw a topcoat in my face. I cleared the ball and I had to pick up the topcoat and bring it back to the net. Another shot came in. I blocked it again, and they threw a cap in my face. But I cleared the ball again. They were throwing stuff in on top of my head. I looked back with about three minutes to go and wasn't the back of the net gone. The very minute the match as over I walked out a bit and the Cork forwards and the Tipperary backs ran down and saved me. I had to stay on the pitch for two hours. They had twenty around me. I wanted to go but they wouldn't let me go.'

Tony Reddin, on the 1950 Munster final, quoted in Colm Keane, *Hurling's Top Twenty* (2002).

'You can say what you like but the only team you can hurl all out against is Tipperary.'

Christy Ring, quoted in Breandán Ó hEithir, *Over the Bar* (1984).

'At the end of an hour's brutality in the Tipp vs Cork replay, Paddy Leahy asked Lynch what he thought about extra time. "I have enough of it," said Jack.'

Anecdote from 1949 Munster final, quoted by Tipperary writer Raymond Smith.

'Jimmy Kennedy would go over to the sideline and he tied up his shoes. He kept away from Kilkenny by ten yards and they didn't go near him. The very minute I pucked the ball to him he got a lovely hop and snapped it over the bar. The goalie later said to me, "That was a mighty puck, you've got great eyes."'

Tony Reddin, Tipperary goalkeeper from the 1950s, quoted in Colm Keane, *Hurling's Top Twenty* (2002).

'Steven Segal plays the part of 1984 Tipp goalkeeper John Sheedy. Segal had to spend four weeks of intensive training on blocking down balls going over the bar for opposing forwards to score goals just like Sheedy did for Seánie O'Leary of Cork in the 1984 Munster Final. If anyone has forgotten, Tipp led 3–14 to 2–13 with four minutes to go, but Sheedy's errors made it 4–15 to 3–14 for Cork.'

Weblog, *Tipperary, the Movie*.

'Players would be dropped off the panel whether they deserved it or not; managers would change for much the same reason and the whole depressing cycle continued.'

Pat Fox, Tipperary hurler from the 1980s.

'The days when Tipp supporters go to a game expecting to win easily, are the days that Tipp are traditionally most vulnerable.'

Nicky English, pre-match speech.

'The famine is over.'

Richard Stakelum, Tipperary captain (1987).

'It seems mad now but I went out that evening and played a challenge for my club against Holycross. Then I made a dash home to watch the match on *The Sunday Game*. And the next morning I was up at seven o'clock to draw in hay. Whatever about the Munster final, the bales still had to be brought into the hayshed. I got no special dispensation.'

John McIntyre, on the 1984 final between Tipperary and Cork.

'A great lurching twister of a season blew itself out at Croke Park. When it counted Tipperary were the only team still standing. Yes, Tipperary the old bluebloods of hurling. They

took their 25th title with a margin of three points and none has been harder fought or better deserved.'
Tom Humphries, on the 2001 All-Ireland, *The Irish Times*.

'Honours For English.'
Irish Independent headline, paying tribute to the Tipperary manager in 2001.

'Tipperary's 25th crown did not come from splashy, extrovert hurling. It came from a compound of abstract forces. From intimate things. Like faith. And loyalty. More than anything, perhaps, fear.'
Vincent Hogan, *Irish Independent.*

'The ball bounced off me, came off Kevin, rolled wide and we win an All-Ireland. That is how close it can be between winning and losing.'
Brendan Commins, Tipperary goalkeeper, quoted in the *Irish Independent.*

'There is no secret. It is all learning. Our last couple of years, drawing a game we should have won, hammered in the replay, coming back to a Munster final, getting caught up in the hype, not really performing, being individual instead of being a team. Then, going into last year's quarter-final still on the crest of the wave, not absorbing that we had lost in Munster and being individual. Our only job is to make sure that these lessons are passed on. The big moments are between the lines.'
Nicky English, quoted in *The Irish Times*.

'There were times when Tipperary had some of their players beaten, but as a team they performed better than Galway and that was the main difference. They were under pressure in the second half but they kept their heads when Galway came hardest at them. And throughout the game, they were picking off their scores with greater ease, whereas Galway always seemed to be working extremely hard to get their scores.'

Eamonn Cregan, inter-county hurling manager, *The Irish Times*.

'For Tipperary manager Nicky English, there have been many many moments in a hurling career that twice glittered with All-Ireland gold, but Sunday's All-Ireland final victory by his young charges will surely eclipse the lot.'

Diarmuid O'Flynn, *Irish Examiner*.

'It would be unfair if Leahy was remembered for that.'

Michael Keating, on John Leahy's highly publicised contretemps with a Limerick supporter, Steven Downey, in a pub in Manchester (1996).

'He gets under your skin in a variety of ways. On the days when he's on song the ball seems to find him, he's like a magnet for the ball.'

Tom Helebert, on John Leahy.

'There is the idea that he is a bit of a boyo, he must be a bit of a pup. I think it's unfair. He has an aggressive side, but every hurler needs what he has.'

Conor O'Donovan, on John Leahy.

'Leahy is recognised now as the people's champion, with un-limited horizons opening up before him.'
Tipperary writer Raymond Smith, *Sunday Independent* (7 June 1992).

'Declan [Ryan] would have had no problem scoring himself. If anything he was treating me as an old cripple by holding on to the ball so long to set me up in a scoring position. So, having scored, I looked across at him and grinned. I felt as if he was helping me like you'd help an invalid. If anything, I felt that he was having a bit of a laugh at me.'
Nicky English, on the 1993 Munster final.

Tyrone

'We had to beat 31 and a half counties.'
Mick O'Dwyer on the 1986 All-Ireland final.

'It'll change our lives forever, today we're made men.'
John Devine of Tyrone, on the 2003 All-Ireland final.

'I wonder how it would have been projected if ourselves and Kerry had served up the greatest spectacle of high scor-ing football and we lost. Then it would have been said that Tyrone are a great footballing team but they can't win. There's no use in us playing flamboyantly and losing.'
Mickey Harte, on the 2003 All-Ireland semi-final.

'When Meath put it up to us physically, we should have taken them on at their own game and if that meant having a row, so be it. Instead, we looked to the referee for protection.

Allowed ourselves to be divided, and then picked off. Afterwards, we should have retreated, said nothing, licked our
wounds, learned from our mistakes and stayed together to set
the record straight in 1997. Instead, the team fell apart.'
Ciaran McBride.

'Tyrone are an extremely talented side, why they feel the
need to be ultra-defensive I don't know. Personally, I'd like to
see them express themselves.'
Paddy Collins, former chairman of the National Referees
Committee.

'It was intense, but not one Kerry player had to leave that
field injured. If anything was injured, it was Kerry's pride.'
Mickey Harte, on the 2003 All-Ireland semi-final.

'The first time I got the ball I passed it to a team-mate and
raced to take the return pass but instead he booted the ball
two miles in the air.'
Iggy Jones, Tyrone footballer from the 1950s.

'Well he was a young lad who died doing something he loved.
Playing football for his county and enjoying himself.'
Priest who saw Paul McGirr before his death in a tragic
football accident playing for Tyrone minors.

'I think it has been a real basis for the character of these lads
that are now in the senior team. They've grown together.
They did a lot of growing in a short space of time. And
although it's human nature that people move on and get on
with their own lives long after something happens, I think

there's a lasting bond there. It's a hidden thing that nobody really talks about but certainly a number of the players are aware of it. There was an unwritten pact to say, "Let's go forward from here and do the best we can." And maybe, just maybe out there, there's a Paul McGirr factor without anybody making a deal of it.'

Mickey Harte, Tyrone manager.

'For over 100 years that trophy had been the holy grail of every Gaelic games supporter in Tyrone. But here, amid such grief, its presence was scarcely noticed.'

Ciaran McBride, on the funeral of Cormac McAnallen.

Waterford

'Best of luck, and don't make a hash of it this time.'

Jack Lynch, talking to Waterford's Mick Hayes in 1948, quoted in Brendan Fullam, *Legends of the Ash* (1997).

'Tipp and Cork have tradition. We have tradition too. A tradition of keeping going.'

Pat Fanning of Waterford, during preparations for 1957 All-Ireland final.

'Training was done in Walsh Park in front of an attendance that would do justice to a county championship match. They were there night after night, drinking in the atmosphere, talking and arguing and wondering what was to be.'

Pat Fanning of Waterford, on the build up to the 1948 All-Ireland final, quoted in Colm Keane, *Hurling's Top Twenty* (2002).

Westmeath

'If everyone got up and left their roots to chase success, there would be no GAA.'

David Kilcoyne of Westmeath.

'A victory for guts and heart and determination.'

Colm O'Rourke, after Westmeath won the Leinster title for the first time in 2004.

'Westmeath blew into a nine-point lead ahead of Meath during the opening 20 minutes of their All-Ireland quarter-final game. They were playing the best football seen anywhere this summer. Then they remembered themselves.'

Tom Humphries, *The Irish Times*.

'What Westmeath's progress this year has shown above all is the travesty that was the old-style championship for over 100 years. Thankfully, things will never be the same again.'

Eugene McGee, *Irish Independent*.

Wexford

'Of all the Wexford folk, who threatened suicide or, at the very least, serious mutilation of self or selector after defeat by Offaly in the '84 Leinster final, do not 99 per cent now reminisce about that as the ill year of Doran's resistless late fetch and fulminating shot and goal and all his other gaiscí that brought low the double double Cats?'

Kevin Cashman (25 April 1993).

'They used to say of Skinny Meara from Tipp that he could stop a swallow flying through a barn door. Fitzhenry makes swallows give up wanting to fly through barn doors.'

Tom Humphries, on Wexford goalkeeper Damien Fitzhenry, *The Irish Times* (5 July 2004).

'We had lost titles when were four points up. We had given games away easily because we had lost our concentration or didn't stick to the gameplan or allowed D.J. in with a heap of steps for a soft goal. We talked about the Leinster finals in '84 (lost to Offaly by one point) '88, '93 twice and '94 and how we always seemed to come out the wrong side of things. Basically we faced up to the fact that the reason there was always something wrong was our own fault. We promised each other that we were going to win on Sunday. It was the first time since I started playing that the players took responsibility for themselves.'

Martin Storey, Wexford hurler from the 1980s and 1990s.

'The weaker counties may be lost sheep but we must always keep looking out for them because I feel very strongly that the right to play hurling is a cultural thing that must be respected.'

George O'Connor, Wexford hurler from the 1980s and 1990s.

'I have heard a lot of questions asked about Wexford these last few years and I don't mind saying that I am proud to have Wexford blood in my veins. I want you to be proud to be Wexford people. Of all the counties in this country for people to suggest that there's something wrong with the blood in our veins, this is not one of them. History tells you who you are. We are from Wexford, from the Blackstairs Mountains to Fethard, back to Rosslare and all the way as far as Gorey and Arklow in the north.'

Liam Griffin, Wexford hurling manager from the 1990s.

'Welcome to *Planet of the Wexfords*, the surprise hit of the summer now showing on a pitch near you. Like its counterpart, *Planet of the Apes*, the key to this blockbuster is the surprise ending which shows you've been watching something completely different to what initially seemed to be the case.'

Eamonn Sweeney, *Irish Examiner*.

'Wexford of course has traditionally been known as the Model County but don't go there expecting to find the likes of the leggy Christy Turlington or Elizabeth Hurley ready to take a whack at your sliotar.'

Brendan Breathnach.

'I actually cried when I read about us being bridesmaids and yellowbellies.'

Liam Griffin, Wexford hurling manager from the 1990s.

'Asking Wexford manager Tony Dempsey how he intends to approach this evening's replay is about as practical as instructing an eel to stop wriggling.'

Vincent Hogan, *Irish Independent*.

'On a weekend football's pussycats played to plan, the old relics of Vinegar Hill chose to bare their dentures. And get a load of how they did it. Martin Storey was excavated from some museum in Oulart, given a hearing-aid and a jersey, told that life begins at 37. Larry O'Gorman was dragged from the bridge table and thrown towards a skateboard; Liam Dunne got pressed into a bold safari once he'd proved he could still count a paramedic's fingers. What next? Maybe we'll spring Billy Byrne or Tom Dempsey... Who knows, perhaps old George even.'

Tony Dempsey, manager, quoted by Vincent Hogan, *Irish Independent.*

'There is something pigheaded about Wexford this season though, something pigheaded and perverse and oddly beautiful. They were wounded badly in the Leinster final but ever since they keep staggering into shot, stealing other people's lines, causing mayhem. In certain lights they are starting to look heroic.'

Tom Humphries, *The Irish Times.*

'If Wexford Hurling Ltd was a company and we had produced the results that we have over the last 25 years or so, we would have been declared bankrupt long ago.'

Phil Murphy, *Wexford People.*

Wicklow

'I often wonder if we changed the names of counties and jersey colours and started all over again, would it make a difference?'

Kevin O'Brien, Wicklow footballer from the 1980s.

And Finally:

A Word from the ArchBish

The Palace, Thurles, 18 December 1884

My Dear Sir, I beg to acknowledge the receipt of your communication inviting me to become a patron of the Gaelic Athletic Association, of which you are it appears, the Hon. Secretary. I accede to your request with the utmost pleasure. One of the most painful, let me assure you, and at the same time, one of the most frequent recurring, reflections that, as an Irishman, I am compelled to make in connection with the present aspect of things in this country, is derived from the ugly and irritating fact that we are daily importing from England, not only her manufactured goods, which we cannot help doing, since she has practically strangled our own manufacturing appliances, but together with her fashions, her accents, her vicious literature, her music, her dances, and her manifold mannerisms, her games also, and her pastimes, to the utter discredit of our own grand national sports, and to the sore humiliation, as I believe, or every genuine son and daughter of the old land. Ball-playing, hurling, football-kicking according to Irish rules, 'casting', leaping in various ways, wrestling, handy-grips, top-pegging, leap-frog, rounders, tipin-the-hat, and all such favourite exercises and amusements amongst men and boys may now be said to be not only dead and buried, but in several localities to be entirely forgotten and unknown. And what have we got in their stead? We have got such foreign and fantastic field sports as lawn tennis, polo, croquet, cricket, and the like – very excellent, I believe, and health-giving exercises in their way, still not racy of the soil, but rather alien, on the contrary, to it, as are indeed, for the most part, the men and women who first imported, and still continue to patronize them. And, unfortunately, it is not our national sports alone that are held in dishonor and are dying out, but even our most suggestive national celebrations are being gradually effaced and extinguished, one after another as well, who hears now of snap-apple night, pan-cake night, or bon-fire night? They are all things of the past, too vulgar to be spoken of except in ridicule by the degenerate dandies of the day. No doubt, there is something rather pleasing to the eye in the get-up of the modern man who, arrayed in light attire, with parti-coloured cap on and a racquet in hand, making his way, with or without a companion, to the tennis ground. But, for my part, I should vastly prefer to behold, or think of, the youthful athletes whom I used to see in my early days at fair and pattern, bereft of shoes and coat, and thus prepared to play at handball, to fly over any number of horses, to throw the 'sledge', or 'winding-stone', and to test each other's mental activity by the trying ordeal of 'three leaps', or a 'hop, step and jump'. Indeed if we continue travelling for the next score years in the same direction that we have been going in for some time past, condemning the sports that were practised by our forefathers, effacing our national features as though we were ashamed of them, and putting on, with England's stuffs and broadcoats, her masher habits and such other effeminate follies as she may recommend, we had better at once, and publicly, abjure our nationality, clap hands for joy at the sight of the Union Jack, and place 'England's bloody red' exultantly above the green. Depreciating as I do any sure dire and disgraceful consummation, and seeing in your society of athletes something altogether opposed to it, I shall be happy to do all for it that I can, and authorize you now formally to place my name on the roll of your patrons. In conclusion, I earnestly hope that our national journals will not disdain in future to give suitable notices of these Irish sports and pastimes which your society means to patronize and promote, and that the masters and pupils of our Irish Colleges will not henceforth exclude from their athletic programmes such manly exercises as I have just referred to and commemorated. I remain, my dear Sir, your very faithful servant.